DR JACK

DR JACK

CALCUTTA'S
PAVEMENT DOCTOR

JEREMY JOSEPHS

BLOOMSBURY

First published in Great Britain 1991
Bloomsbury Publishing Limited, 2 Soho Square, London W1V 5DE

PICTURE SOURCES

Marcel Crozet/Visage du Monde/Calcutta Rescue   page 6 *top*
Mark McEvoy   page 6 *bottom*
Helene Rogers   page 7 *bottom*, page 8
Royal College of Surgeons, Dublin   page 3 *top*
Bob Turner   page 7 *top*

A CIP catalogue record for this book
is available from the British Library

ISBN 0-7475-0890-9

10 9 8 7 6 5 4 3 2 1

Typeset by Rowland Phototypesetting Limited
Bury St Edmunds, Suffolk
Printed by Butler and Tanner Limited, Frome and London

For the destitutes of Calcutta

Contents

Preface

The idea for this book began life rather inauspiciously in a black plastic dustbin liner. What happened was that my wife began to talk about an article she had read in the *Sunday Times*, but only once the papers had been disposed of. She told me the story of the STREET DOCTOR IN CALCUTTA WHO FACES JAIL. Anxious to find a subject for my next book, I retrieved the piece and immediately knew that Jack Preger was it. I think I was attracted towards his story because of my long-standing interest in the twin issues of Jewishness and human rights, which for me have always been inextricably bound up with the Holocaust. And the life story of Jack Preger, once an orthodox Jew – and now, perhaps, a Messianic Jew again – is all about the quest for human rights. However, any common ground between us ends here. For whereas Jack has been working with the destitutes of Bengal for almost twenty years now, I saw my role, more modestly, as putting on record the achievements of this most remarkable man.

Before leaving for Calcutta in the autumn of 1989, I conducted extensive interviews with Jack's former wives, family and friends. In fact by the time I boarded the Air India jumbo I was convinced that I knew more about him than he knew about himself. What I had found out, though, before meeting 'Saint Jack', as many a journalist has referred to him, was that he was not quite the saint he was purported to be. Things were a good deal more confused, for I discovered a casualty list of women and children who had been left behind as Jack blazed his amazing trail out East. So it was with some trepidation that I travelled to Calcutta's Middleton Row, unsure if Jack would cooperate with me at all. But when I arrived at the clinic, and Jack greeted me with the immortal words: 'I've been a bastard – write what you like', I knew immediately that I was unlikely to encounter any such difficulties. And what a sense of humour. I loved Jack's suggestion for the title of this book, revealed in subsequent correspondence between us: *The Story of a Nutter in Calcutta*. In my view there is no greater gift than being able to laugh at yourself.

Keeping up with Jack was no easy task. In fact, the day before I submitted my manuscript, a ten-page letter arrived informing me that one clinic was opening and another was closing, and that while registration was a little nearer, funding for the clinic was as problematic as ever. I'm just wondering whether or not this was what I refer to later as 'another Preger prank'. And I dare say that, come publication day, things are likely to have moved on again. It's the age-old problem of a moving target.

I have changed the names of a few people featured in this book. Once, because I was asked to do so; and on a couple of other occasions because I thought it appropriate. Other than that, every-thing I have written is true, although needless to say any mistakes are of my own making.

A proportion of the proceeds of this book will go to the Calcutta Rescue Fund, the Preger support group that is active in the UK and sent over £100,000 to Calcutta in 1989. A full list of contact names and addresses is given on pages 185–6.

There are so many people to thank for their help that I shall just list their names rather than specify the precise manner in which each assisted me. It's a little like putting a jigsaw together: had any of the following names been missing, the picture would have been in-complete. So I would like to express my appreciation to Jonathan D. Rose, Diane Booth, Frances Meigh, Chaim Neslen, John Justice, Helene Rogers and Bob Turner, the Basu family in Calcutta, Suzanne Franks, Kevin Mulley, Anita Ostrin, Leslie Preger, Shaemus Cunnane, Cathy and John McGregor, Antonia Walder,

Preface

Maritta Preger, Allen Jewhurst, Ben Kingsley and all members of the Josephs and Frank families.

Whether or not I should thank my wife Clair for encouraging me to retrieve that article from the bin, I really don't know. Because by so doing she was in effect giving me an enormous amount of work, which took almost two years to complete. But if I have suffered, she did too, as I inflicted one rewrite after another on her.

In the unpublished foreword to Frances Meigh's book, *The Jack Preger Story*, Jack wrote: 'This is not, thank goodness, a biography; and much has been omitted. Because biographies ought to be kept for the "twilight" years or even later.'

I'm glad that I managed to persuade Jack to change that view. For this is, for better or worse, a biography, and nothing, to the best of my knowledge and abilities, has been omitted. On the streets of Calcutta, to lepers, destitutes and patients alike, Jack is known, delightfully, as Dr Jack. This is his story.

Jeremy Josephs
Summer 1991

Foreword

A useful rule of thumb for those of us fortunate (or unfortunate) enough to be relatively well known to the public is that the vast majority of requests to embrace worthy causes – however deserving – should be turned down. For one thing, there is simply not the time to endorse every compelling cause that is brought to your attention, and for another, there is the danger of cheapening your own currency. So when Jeremy Josephs first approached me with a view to my writing the foreword to *Dr Jack: Calcutta's Pavement Doctor*, it was with precisely this somewhat starchy, if sensible, justification that I declined.

I am now, with hindsight, delighted that Jeremy Josephs proved so much more persistent than many of his fellow petitioners. For he has succeeded in demonstrating, both in our correspondence and in this most powerful biography, the uniqueness of Jack Preger, a man whose devotion to the destitutes of Calcutta must make him a highly eligible candidate for the Nobel Peace Prize. Mother Teresa has, quite rightly, long been fêted by the international community, and has received a host of prizes and accolades. The time is surely ripe for the invaluable pioneering work of Dr Jack to be paid similar tribute.

Unlike Dr Jack, I have not devoted the greater part of my life to helping the poorest of the poor. But I am no stranger to India; India is in my blood. When Sir Richard Attenborough asked me, in the early 1980s, to play the leading role in his film *Gandhi*, I relished the opportunity, and threw myself into the part, reading countless biographies and ploughing through most of Gandhi's own writings, which include twenty-three volumes of collected works and an autobiography. I learned a lot about Gandhi. And I am certain that he would wholeheartedly have given his blessing both to Dr Jack Preger and to this truly first-class account of his life and work.

Ben Kingsley

1

Pog Mo Thoin!

Middleton Row is posh. It is one of the best addresses in Calcutta. The street is dominated by the spire of the city's smartest private girls' school: Loreto House, a building once occupied by the first Chief Justice of the Supreme Court of Calcutta. Yet it is here that mothers clutching emaciated babies and children with leprosy and tuberculosis queue daily to receive medical help. For over a decade now there has been a street clinic in Middleton Row, and for much of that time it has functioned in spite of official disapproval. Its patients, destitute for the most part, have come to see the British doctor who runs the clinic.

A street clinic for the destitute sits rather uneasily in Middleton Row. For in more than one respect the Row is home to Calcutta's establishment. This was not decided or decreed as an act of deliberate policy or planning, for that is not the way things happen in Calcutta. Rather the area just evolved that way. A few yards from Loreto House there stands each day an armed guard in full military attire, charged with protecting property belonging to the Royal Calcutta Turf Club. The street also houses innumerable plush offices, some of which are immediately adjacent to the clinic. The Catholic Association of Bengal is also nearby. The British doctor, however, is by no means part of this comfortable Calcuttan clique.

It is outside this formidable array of buildings that a constant stream of destitute and dying patients arrive on a first-come first-served basis. Examinations are carried out free of charge — one of the reasons why the clinic has proved so popular. This 'clinic' is in reality a narrow ribbon of pavement six feet wide, with only a series of makeshift tarpaulins to protect it from the elements. There is usually at least one queue of patients stretching several hundred yards. These people are the poor pavement-dwellers of Calcutta. Most are anxious to see the grey-haired doctor from overseas.

In many respects the clinic is like any general medical practice anywhere in the world, with patients suffering from endless coughs and colds, headaches, pains and fevers. And yet in as many respects there is really no other clinic quite like Middleton Row. For daily there are to be found countless children suffering from a wide variety of sexually transmitted diseases; cripples from polio; victims of amputation by ruthless begging syndicates; hundreds of untreated lepers; cases of cholera; abdominal distensions, malaria and elephantiasis. Almost all of the patients are malnourished or have worms. To Western eyes, it is a numbing, scarcely credible sight.

These destitutes come to Middleton Row because there is no free hospital for the city's poor. The small quota of free beds in the hospitals are taken up by those who have addresses and ration cards and can afford to pay for diagnoses. At College State Hospital, for example, patients wait in corridors because wards are overflowing. Some time ago one patient, a pavement-dweller by the name of Sabir, had a gangrenous foot that needed amputation as a matter of urgency. He was sent from Middleton Row to College State Hospital with a letter requesting surgery. Refused admission, he ended up sleeping in the hospital grounds. By the time he had found his way back to Middleton Row the tendons of his leg were exposed and there were dozens of maggots gnawing away at the limb. This infuriated the British doctor. But it did not surprise him. Being the victims of bungling, corruption and neglect is an everyday occurrence for the poor and needy of Calcutta.

At the Middleton Row clinic there is usually a team of half a dozen salaried Indian doctors to attend to patients. Funding comes from charitable donations given by well-wishers overseas. The doctors are supported by a team of energetic volunteers, most of whom are likewise from foreign countries. All of them have heard of the British doctor's work and have been inspired by it. Some of the volunteers working on the Row are qualified in nursing; the majority are not. Their backgrounds have ranged from accountancy to zoology and just about everything in between. Many are students, but there was even a Swedish judge. More often than not there is a hard core of Irish volunteers. All the volunteers have been prepared to give a short period of their lives, normally some three to six months, or until visa problems are encountered, in order to help the pavement-dwellers of Calcutta.

The voluntary workers are well aware that their contributions, however well intentioned, are purely transitory, amounting to a few months here and a few months there. But it is always worthwhile. The British doctor, though, has been working in the Third World for over two decades now. He has seen hundreds of volunteers come and go. The doctor's name is Jack, and he has had more than the odd skirmish with the powers that be. His relationship with the authorities is a little better now, but his instincts remain firmly anti-establishment. Completely dedicated to his patients, he never ceases to amaze. One past volunteer, Dr Sarah Sallon, recalls her impressions thus:

> He's got this terrific conviction that he's doing the right thing. It's a religious conviction with him – that he must continue to do it. And people like that are like iron. They don't give up. They drop dead in their tracks, mind you, but they don't give up. These are people who are great pioneers and crusaders, who lead revolutions and, in Jack's case, run a street clinic. They're unusual. You don't come across them so often.

Jack is certainly unusual. He is the first to admit it. And so is the clinic that he runs. The approach of the volunteers, however, is entirely pragmatic. It has to be. There is an unspoken resolve not to dwell on the enormity of the suffering and to focus all energy on the task in hand. Middleton Row might well be a street clinic, but it does not dispense shoddy goods. On the contrary, its standard of dressings remains so consistently high that a Calcuttan professor of leprology actually sends his own patients there. Care and compassion are the hallmarks of the clinic. For Middleton Row is one of the few places in Calcutta prepared to treat lepers, who are widely regarded as outcasts. For many years now, some of the country's top medical posts relating to the treatment of leprosy have remained vacant because doctors and researchers alike are simply not interested in working in that particular field, even though there is a desperate need for their services. There is no glamour or prestige about leprosy; and certainly no money in it. Yet Jack has actively sought out lepers as patients, aware that if the disease is diagnosed early enough medication can virtually stop it in its tracks.

To many of the volunteers Middleton Row presents a bemusing and baffling challenge. Many find the conditions of the clinic too cramped and claustrophobic. Unable to work on the grubby pavement with its infinite assortment of ants, mosquitoes, bugs and other insects, they move on. Others stick the course. Diane Rayner, a nursing sister from St James's Hospital in Leeds, spent almost six months working there:

> When I first came obviously I was really shocked, having just come out of an NHS hospital where everything is very sterile and very clean – and where everyone knows what's wrong with a patient. Here, you just have to get on with it and do the best you can. And if you haven't got something you need, you use a substitute, which at first I found quite difficult. But now you just get on with it.

The reality of 'getting on with it' has entailed, in the past, using gardening gloves when dressing patients suffering from syphilis, in an improvised attempt to ward off infection. Another volunteer, Antonia Walder, a law graduate from London, had her eyes opened rather wider than she would have wished:

> Most of the dressings which we prepared were for lepers' stumps, which were constantly getting infected. Their limbs often just get in the way – they lose all feeling, and rats will gnaw at them. I had only been working in Middleton Row for a few days when a

leper once asked me to cut his toe off, since he had no use for it anymore. Fortunately Jack decided that there was still some circulation in it so he should keep it for a while longer. Though I was fast getting over any squeamishness, I would not have relished the task.

The term 'street clinic' makes it all sound rather like a market-stall approach to medicine. It is certainly true that the card-index system, the medicines and tarpaulin covers alike all arrive at the beginning of each day and have gone again by the time the patients have been seen, usually late in the afternoon. A patch of pavement by night, Middleton Row metamorphoses into an outdoor medical practice by day. But in terms of the product provided, any similarities with a street market are entirely invalid. The clinic is highly organized, with a series of different 'departments' designed to meet patients' needs and including a 'dressing station', 'pharmacy', 'finance' and 'indexation'. The workers of Middleton Row are aware that there has always been profound poverty in Calcutta, and that the chances are that there always will be, however great their efforts. One way to deal with this immense obstacle and the all too evident suffering is to seize on the lighter moments of street life. Seldom is there any shortage of material. Anne, an Irish volunteer from Dublin who has returned several times to work in the clinic, recalls:

> The patients are great fun. Often they have no idea of their age. There was one chap who we sent for surgery who told me he was fifty. We checked this with him prior to the operation and this time he said eighty. So we cross-examined him on this and he eventually conceded: 'Well, somewhere between fifty and eighty.'

Jack can laugh, too. He has a reputation for his sharp sense of humour. Most of the volunteers will tell you that Jack is nothing but fun to work with. In fact the humour provides a veil beneath which a good deal of anger is successfully disguised from friend and foe alike. For Jack knows that in Calcutta there are private medical institutions that can rival anything offered in the West. The city's

Belle Vue clinic, for example, boasts facilities that are difficult to surpass. It is part of a flourishing private health sector supported by India's middle classes. This gulf between the haves and the have-nots exists in every city in the world, but nowhere is it more pronounced than in Calcutta. The British doctor – Jack Preger is his full name – has set out to remedy this injustice. Not that he is the first to have detected the unpleasant odour of boundless inequality. The writer Geoffrey Moorhouse had this to say about Calcutta before the good doctor had even thought of setting foot on Indian soil:

> For this is a very wealthy city as well as a squalidly poor one and the two elements live so close together, they present such grotesque contrasts, the one has so frequently begotten the other, that anger is the most natural and the healthiest response in the world. In a sense, Calcutta is a definition of obscenity.

Moorhouse may have visited India before Preger, but John Gunther was there even earlier. Writing shortly before the outbreak of the Second World War, he recorded this impression of the city:

> The *bustees* (hovels) of the jute workers of Calcutta are worse than anything in Poland, worse than Naples and Glasgow or even Shanghai. Workers getting three or four rupees a week live in cells with no light, no water, no sanitation; the entrance to the hovels is a tunnel streaming with sewage; nine to ten people may live in rooms eight feet by six. Disease, squalor, degradation of the human being to the level of animals are rampant, as men live in stinking filth.

Günter Grass, Salman Rushdie and Dominique Lapierre are more recent writers who have been horrified by Calcutta, though little has changed for all their protestations. For the destitute of Calcutta things go on much as before. True, most of the jute mills have long since closed. But a series of disasters – some acts of God, some man-made – have served only to compound the formidable array of problems besetting the city. In fact the problem is simply stated:

6

Calcutta is home to too many people. Originally designed for a population of one million, the city now swells with almost fifteen times that amount. In the four decades since Independence its population has more than doubled. People keep coming to Calcutta in the hope of a better future. Some are from the countryside; many others are from Bangladesh. A West Bengali Finance Minister once complained: 'If you improve things, that only brings in more from outside.' And in many respects he was right. It is an enormous, sprawling, seething mass of humanity, bursting at the seams. Not surprisingly, something has had to give. More often than not it is the health of the city's poor.

The medical details of every patient attending Jack Preger's clinic are put on file. Almost twenty thousand names appear on these lists. But since the majority of patients are pavement-dwellers, their addresses must surely rank among the oddest ever held on medical record. Typical entries read: 'the foot of the third lamp-post', 'by central concrete pillar', 'opposite the *thana*' (police station), 'under Howrah Bridge north', 'at foot of steps southside'.

Half the population of Calcutta live in rundown houses, or delapidated *bustees*. Yet these are among the more fortunate; they at least have an address. More than a million others live on nothing more elaborate than the street. They attempt to eke out an existence in concrete nooks and crannies, on disused railway lines, every-where, under canvas, sacks or nothing, surrounded by fetid filth and indifferent passers-by. Sometimes they are successful and survive; sometimes not.

For the poor of Calcutta there is precious little dignity, even in death. Rarely can they afford to be cremated, and many corpses are simply dropped quietly into the Hooghly. Since this is a tributary of the holy Ganges, its qualities are said to compensate in part for not burning the body. In fact the problem of dropping unwanted corpses into the Ganges has become so widespread that thousands of blind, flesh-eating scavenger turtles have been released into its waters in the hope that they will consume the unwanted bodies of the recently departed poor.

Many of the patients of the Middleton Row clinic were born and brought up on the pavements of Calcutta, and lived their whole lives and sometimes died on the streets. There have been marriages in which a proud father's dowry to his daughter was the best piece of pavement on the block to share with her prospective partner. Schools for the children of such unions are conducted on the pavements. Miserable slabs of paving stones have been fought over, squatted on and defended with such energy and vigour that one might be excused for thinking that these were battles relating to the very highest of high finance.

It is as well that the volunteers working in Middleton Row have limited objectives. Aware that the odds against them are formidable, the Irish nurse Anne describes her motivation in this way:

> I didn't come away thinking that I was going to change the world. I simply think that these people are getting very good medical care here on the Row and they get an opportunity to get their diseases treated – often TB and leprosy – which many of the government hospitals won't touch with a bargepole. The clinic is very well organized by Jack. Nor is there any religious element in this work at all. We just get stuck in. And I say that anything you can do for anyone else is a good thing.

The reputation of the clinic is high. Every day forty to fifty new patients arrive. And every day three to four hundred patients are attended to. Sometimes patients get more than they bargained for. For in addition to the provision of medical attention, one of the volunteers will ensure that the money received by the clinic is distributed to patients. Two to five rupees per patient is usual, but it varies according to each individual's personal circumstances. Each patient also receives four biscuits, a packet of *satu*, a packet of *dal*, and every second visit they are also allocated half a bar of soap. There is no doubt that some patients fabricate complaints in order to benefit from the provisions freely handed out by the clinic, but volunteers soon become expert in distinguishing between the needy and the greedy.

The clinic is open for business six days a week, closing on Sunday. Patients begin to arrive at about five or six in the morning to be towards the front of the queue. Medical attention normally gets under way at 8.30 a.m. Many patients will have come in order to take advantage of the 'baby clinic', which closely monitors babies' weight and provides extra nutrition if necessary. And overseeing all of these complex transactions – financial, medical, social, administrative and pharmaceutical; attending to the needs of the volunteers; dealing with queries from the salaried doctors; and rushing up and down and all over Middleton Row with much energy and vigour is the man who conceived, created and has fought for the right of that street clinic to exist. Jack Preger is a man who continues to speak up for the poor and downtrodden of Calcutta in spite of repeated attempts to silence him. It is not surprising that patients and workers alike are more than a little impressed. Diane Rayner, the nurse from Leeds, certainly was:

As long as you live you'll never meet another person like Jack. He is really someone quite outstanding. I just don't know how he carries on. It's a bit like having a saint amongst you – the way he walks up and down – it's just like having a living saint.

Another volunteer, John Wiseman, a biochemist from the north of England, was not bowled over quite so easily:

I certainly don't think of Jack as a saint, as many people do. Goodness me, his language is probably the most colourful of all of us. He'll have no hesitation in telling somebody to fuck off. You'll often hear him yelling his head off at those out to cause mischief on the Row. And he certainly likes his pint of Guinness, although it's hard to get the stuff out here.

Impressing idealistic young volunteers from the West is one thing, but impressing the streetwise poor of the East is quite another. If anything, though, Jack's patients tend to be even more gushing with their praise. M. D. Safwi, for example, is a former patient and now an employee at Middleton Row. He is usually one of the first to arrive, as it is his task to erect the tarpaulin covers and to fetch water. He is one of twenty or so local staff. He works with a man by the name of Devanand who has polio in both legs and who makes paper packets from *raddi*, from which medicines are dispensed and distributed. Neither is in any doubt: 'Doctor is our god.' Parallels between Preger and the Almighty are frequently hinted at, if not always articulated. Sometimes grateful patients attempt to show their reverence by holding an umbrella over their Doctor-God to shield him from the searing Calcuttan sun.

Does Preger hold such an elevated view of his own work?

A lot of the things that people imagine about somebody like myself are just projected fantasies. The fact is that I happen to work with poor people. To me it's the most natural thing in the world. If I know a certain amount about medicine, why fight to get a job at home when people need what little medical knowledge or skill I've got so much more? But you do get a lot of this demigod stuff. One Indian journalist once made a rather unfortunate spelling mistake when writing about me, exclaiming, 'Behold the Demi God sitting on his tool in Middleton Row', which went down rather well with the volunteers, as you can imagine. I'm over sixty now – but anyone here who survives above the age of about forty-eight or fifty is considered ancient – and so a familiar saying is 'Behold the venerable stooping figure.' So it's partly a cultural reason that you get such a lot of this ornate language and I really don't take it at all seriously because it's just not true.

Jack Preger has set himself a tough agenda. The battle against TB, for example, which constitutes just part of his work, is itself one of truly Canutine proportions. Not only is tuberculosis India's most widespread illness, it is also its greatest killer disease. Some years ago India's National Institute for Tuberculosis estimated that over two hundred and sixty million of its citizens were exposed to it – and the situation has deteriorated since then. The city's traffic system hardly helps. In fact the word system implies a degree of order that in reality does not exist. For quite apart from the sheer quantity of cars, taxis, buses and vans battling, rattling and bashing their way around the city, with the inevitable chaos of impatient drivers hooting, cursing and sweltering in eternal traffic jams, there are the constant exhaust fumes to contend with. Since many of Preger's patients live on the pavement, they are living at exhaust level.

In Calcutta the air is a lot clearer even five feet above the pavement, although the city still suffers from air pollution levels twice those of Bombay and a third higher than those of Delhi. Annual samples of Calcutta's air have revealed a range of carcinogenic deposits associated chiefly with vehicle emissions. The city's filthy air thus only aggravates the plight of those suffering from TB, and it does no one else much good either. Traffic congestion has become a problem in Middleton Row itself, where taxis in particular come screeching around the corner by Loreto House. In fact this is one of the reasons why Preger is anxious to move the clinic, for there is the distinct possibility that someone might get run over outside, and this might be useful to the authorities, with whom Preger has been battling for some time. A polite notice has therefore been put up: 'Would onlookers kindly refrain from frequenting the road.' On the reverse of this genteel exhortation is written what the saintly doctor from overseas really feels: 'Keep off the fucking road.'

The Middleton Row clinic now concentrates on the diagnosis rather than the treatment of TB. To have attempted to treat all those with the disease would have meant a list of patients running into tens of thousands, something quite beyond the clinic's meagre resources. Once a diagnosis of TB has been firmly established, the preferred course of action is to try to gain for a patient a place in a government TB hospital. But since there are too many people chasing too few beds, seldom is this successful. For when it comes to the allocation of these beds, the poor rootless pavement-dwellers of Calcutta are truly bottom of the pile; and always have been. The clinic's doctors have found that the only solution is to attempt to treat the very seriously ill TB patients as out-patients on the Row – even though the disease will have become 'open' and therefore highly infectious by this stage.

Not that it is such a privilege to be allocated a place in a government hospital. City Hospital, for example, despite being one of West Bengal's main medical centres, has been described by the French writer Dominique Lapierre in these terms:

> Even the most painful visions of the City of Joy had not prepared Margareta for the shock of the sights that awaited her: blood-stained dressings strewn about the corridors, broken beds serving as trash cans, mattresses bursting open and crawling with bugs. Wherever you went you found yourself treading on some form of debris. Worst of all, however, were the people who haunted the place. The severely ill – suffering from encephalitis, coronary thrombosis, tetanus, typhoid, typhus, cholera, infected abscesses, people who had been injured, undergone amputations, or been burned – were lying all over, often on the bare floor.

And yet the spectacle that so troubled Margareta was one of relative privilege. Those patients can again justifiably be described as among the more fortunate of the poor; they had at least been able to pay the bribes invariably demanded before admission by staff at all government hospitals. It is no secret that in India in general and in Calcutta in particular, it is 'salami' (bribes) that makes the world go round. But, bribes aside, there remains a strong antipathy to any patient who cannot provide a satisfactory answer to an apparently straightforward enquiry as to his or her address. A reply such as 'under Howrah Bridge' will just not do.

Yet the prevailing atmosphere in Middleton Row is distinctly optimistic. Another volunteer from Dublin, a teacher named Satty, was understandably proud of a patient with whom she had worked for some time:

> My name is Satty. It is spelled like Fatty. I've been working with this guy, Yosef, for quite a while now. He's from Bangladesh and he came here three years ago. His sister brought him, and he was in a really bad way. He had stood on a bone in the monsoon and this went up into his foot and developed into a bad sinus. Consequently he was unable to walk. When he came here he was as close to dead as made no difference. Jack took an interest in

12

him and brought him back to better health. But for a long time all that was happening was that we were keeping the wound clean, but it wasn't getting any worse or better. The original wound did eventually heal but then he got hit by a taxi here in Calcutta. A lot of our patients here have been involved in road accidents – and if you have seen the way people drive here it is not difficult to see why. Another sinus then developed on Yosef's other leg – and Jack arranged for an orthopaedic surgeon to operate on this one. This made a huge difference. He now wears orthopaedic shoes, which again we arranged for, and calipers because both of his legs were in such a bad condition. When you review the progress he's made, it's been quite remarkable. Because he's gone from not walking at all, to walking with crutches. Then he had an invalid tricycle for a while which was provided by the clinic. Now he just uses a walking stick. So that's not bad going for a man who was close to death's door. I know that anywhere else in the world he would probably have done even better. But given the conditions here I am well pleased.

Yosef's was one of several invalid tricycles coming to and going from Middleton Row. The clinic has provided dozens of disabled patients with these machines. They have become a familiar sight in Calcutta. Most of them have the words 'Calcutta Rescue' painted in bright-red lettering on the back of the vehicle, the name Preger has given to the charities that fund the clinic. Some volunteers have paid for an invalid tricycle from their own savings. Satty certainly did. The dedication that she had inscribed on her particular vehicle might be said to sum up her light-hearted approach to life: *Pog Mo Thoin*, the carriage boldly declares. Since few Calcuttans are familiar with Gaelic, Satty's mother tongue, few complaints have so far been registered with the municipal authorities. But there is no doubt about the translation of the short slogan borne by the rear end of that ramshackle contraption: 'Kiss My Arse'.

There are invariably a number of patients at the clinic who have been involved in road accidents. To successfully negotiate the streets of Calcutta, especially during the rush hour, is an accomplishment not to be underestimated. Other accidents dealt with on the Row are those arising from the work place; there are many cases of burns too. Intestinal parasites and dysentery are also common, especially among the children, many of whom are orphans living on the streets. Yet even they get to hear of Dr Jack's clinic. Many walk several miles, even halfway across Calcutta, because they have heard of his work. Past volunteer Sarah Sallon, a qualified doctor herself, describes the importance to a child of knowing that there is someone in Calcutta who cares:

> There's nobody to look after him – and yet he's managed to stagger across to the clinic and he'll stagger back again to where he sleeps for the night, with his pills, and his medicines and his food. But he knows that Jack's there. He knows that tomorrow he can go again. And he's got a number. He's got that number in his pocket and he'll keep that number, that little token, come rain or hail. And that's very important. That's very important, I think, for people who are displaced, who have no one.

With pitiful stories such as this an everyday occurrence on Middleton Row, it is no surprise that volunteers are constantly scanning the terrain for a little light relief. Nor does one have to be Sigmund Freud to realize that this recurrent need to laugh is an attempt to cope with the constant welter of suffering and deprivation.

More than any other city in the world, Calcutta has always aroused the very strongest of feelings. Nobody is indifferent about Calcutta. The editor of one Indian journal informs readers that 'once you are in love with her, you are trapped'. A publication distributed by the Indian tourist board informs prospective visitors that 'Calcutta loves, Calcutta cares, Calcutta cherishes her own', a slogan that, from Preger's patients' viewpoint, would surely be difficult to surpass for sheer crassness. Others have had a rather different perspective. Winston Churchill, for example, informed his mother: 'I shall always be glad to have seen it – for the same reason Papa gave for being glad to have seen Lisbon – namely, that it will be unnecessary for me ever to see it again.'

And what of Preger? Is he there for the love of Calcutta? Certainly not:

I would love to go somewhere else and retire or take some time off. I have no love for Calcutta and no love for Bengal. The climate is really appalling; for eight or nine months of the year it is totally unbearable.

Why not then pack his bags and return to England?

Because not enough is being done for the poor out here. If it was enough I would be the first one to get out. It's not the actual work that keeps me here, although it often can be interesting and rewarding from a purely medical point of view. It's the principle of the work. These people are denied the help that is available. They are denied it by a government which wants to cover it all up. Of course not everyone would be totally denied medical help if our clinic were to close. A few of the patients would get some kind of help. The point is that they have a moral right to help since help is available and nurses and doctors are available from abroad. The government says no and I say yes.

He is, as one British newspaper headline described him, THE DOCTOR WHO WON'T SHUT UP. Although he has been obliged more recently to modify his position a little, Preger's basic philosophy remains intact, his energy and anger undiminished. What follows is an extract from an article written by him some years ago. It is a devastating indictment of the corruption and inhumanity of Calcutta. 'Salami' has already been referred to, but not as eloquently as this:

The List: we start with 'Salami'. And this is where Grass ought to be at hand, but isn't. Salami in all its variety. So many flavours, all of which are vomit-making. Salami, so many fragrances, all of which stink. For a family, salami to be paid to the police, fifty *paise* bribe, every week, for the indefensible 'right' to lie on a tiny patch of frequently sodden ground closely surrounded by one's fellow rickshaw pullers, push-cart pushers, drug-pushers, smuggled-rice pushers, body-pushers and associated traders, pick-pockets, domestic servants, restaurant hands, street sweepers, scavengers, coolies, beggars, drunks, flop artists, flopped artists, police informers, transvestites (incorporating eunuchs, street entertainers and male-prostitutes), eve-teasers, cock-teasers, cotton-teasers, blood 'donors' (alias sellers), professional recurrently-'sterilized' scrotal skin 'donors' (alias sellers), lunatics, lepers, syphilitics and devotees of other STDs, hepatitics, elephantitics, dysenterics (bacillar and amoebic divisions), the tubercular, the post-poliomyelitic, the malarial, the influenzal, the scabies wallah, ringworm wallah, the lousy, the roundworm, threadworm, whipworm, strongyloides, giardia and trichomonas breeders; the pregnant, the mis-carried, the aborted, the marasmic new-born, the 'nursing' milk-less mothers, the night-blind, the day-and-night blind, the dumb, the catatonic, the deaf, the manic, the walking wounded, the not-so-walking wounded (road traffic accidents, railway accidents, work accidents, knifing accidents, police station *lathi*, rope and boot accidents, and mutilation-for-begging accidents); the drowners and swellers – heart failure, renal failure, liver failure, the pneumonia wallahs, wagon-breakers, car-breakers, house-breakers, ball-breakers, bail-breakers, bicycle-snatchers, chain-snatchers, chain-pullers (railway division), child-snatchers, *mastans*, miscreants, *bodmash*, *goondas*, dacoits in reduced circumstances, anti-social cadres, broken-down-beyond-repair *mistris*, snake charmers, sadhus, monkey wallahs, *misti* wallahs (ear nose throat and wrist departments), nostril piercers and nostril cleaners; ear-lobe piercers and ear-drum piercers, i.e. ear-cleaners; masseurs and manipulators, tight-rope walkers and ritual circumcisers; tabla players and ritual slaughterers (mainly animal); flautists and quacks; fiddlers and pan wallahs; clappers and schleppers; cobblers and toy vendors; barbers and ancillary species of cut-throat specialists, *datura* (stink apple) dispensers and imbibers, vagrants mobile and vagrants immobile (Pickwickian cadre); vagrants legless – choice of left, right, both or partial; vagrants armless, with a similar variety of choices, vagrants eye-less, with more limited choices here; vagrants nose-less . . . and other motley garbage all originally cast in the image

16

of our Creator, allegedly. Now known generically as *CHAM-CHAS* (oilers and greasers).

There has been no shortage of accolades for the doctor's work. And the chances are that more will follow. There have been countless articles about his street clinic in Middleton Row, both nationally and internationally. Many of these have been organized by Preger himself. According to one respected journal he is 'The Unsung Messiah of the Poorest of the Poor'. Whoever he is, Preger has certainly been a thorn in the side of the West Bengal government, which has done its utmost to silence what it perceives as a troublesome, meddling doctor from overseas.

Antonia Walder reports:

A lot of his anger is channelled towards the authorities. He will just refer to them as 'they'. When someone is about to die of TB, for example, or has sold his blood to make ends meet – he'll turn around and, with real venom, say, 'They're real bastards you know.'

Antonia Walder is without doubt a fan; indeed she helps run the UK branch of Calcutta Rescue. Of Preger she says: 'He's a complete and utter hero because he's so down to earth and unassuming and nice. The way he works with patients, his great kindness, is something quite fantastic.'

Jack Preger, for all this, remains a lonely man. Even Antonia returned from her experience in Calcutta to confess that: 'I don't really know what sort of man he is. You go away and you realize that you don't really know anything about him at all.'

Who then is Jack Preger?

2

'He's got the makings of a Rabbi'

Jack Preger is a determined man. It seems that he was a determined foetus too, for he survived a series of attempts by his mother to terminate her pregnancy during its early stages. Some forty years before the appearance on Britain's statute book of the 1967 Abortion Act, Bertha Preger was left with little choice: she was obliged to go through with this unwanted pregnancy and become a mother once again.

However, in reconciling herself to a second child, Bertha Preger remained adamant that this time she would give birth to a girl. A sister for her four-year-old son Leslie would complete the family. Bertha therefore knitted her way through the winter of 1929 and the following spring. By the time she went into labour she was surely as well prepared as any mother could have been, with a formidable range of knitted bootees, sweaters, tops and outfits that would have put less industrious souls to shame. There was just one problem with this impeccable range of infant attire. Most of it was pink, and therefore the wrong colour, as Bertha was about to discover.

For on 25 July 1930, during the late afternoon, Bertha Preger gave birth to a boy. Delivery took place in a room above the grocery shop that Bertha's husband, Harold Louis Preger, owned and ran with a quite remarkable degree of zeal. The shop, H. L. Preger, was situated at 241 Waterloo Road, in the Hightown area of Manchester, in the heart of that city's newly arrived and highly energetic working-class Jewish community. Leslie Preger recalls:

> I remember Jack being born. I didn't really understand what was going on though; it was around closing time in the shop so there weren't many customers around. I was behind the counter with some of the staff when I was told I had a brother. I remember the sense of excitement very clearly.

Bertha Preger was disappointed not to have produced a daughter. But her hopes were not to be dashed quite so easily. The new-born baby might not have sported the clothing painstakingly knitted by his mother, but as a baby and then a toddler Jack was distinctly feminine in appearance. His mother's influence was not difficult to detect. She chose to allow her son's hair, naturally blond and curly, to grow well beyond the accepted length for little boys. When admirers understandably confused boy for girl, Bertha was not at all offended; nor would she seek to put them right. On the contrary, for several years Jack was referred to by mother, father and brother alike as Jackie. It was several years before Bertha would accept that God had given her another son and not the daughter for whom she had hoped and prayed.

Jack was still in his pram when one of his first phrases spilled from his innocent lips. It was assumed that he had picked it up from the women who worked in his father's grocery shop, where the small soul was obliged to spend considerable periods of time. It was a phrase that tickled some folk, but offended many more. For when a would-be admirer, usually another young Jewish mother, paused to comment on the young child's angelic countenance, the pram's tender occupant would not hesitate to produce a terse 'Bugger off'. It is a habit of blunt talking that has remained with Jack ever since.

The Preger family was doing fairly well when Jack was born. Unlike his immigrant wife, Harold Preger was English-born and followed the time-honoured tradition in the Jewish community of going into his father's business. The Pregers' enterprise tended to

19

import many of its groceries, which distinguished it from other local stores of the twenties. As the Pregers prospered, a wholesale side to the business was developed and another outlet was opened. Both shops specialized in importing herrings and cheese, and largely catered to Jewish tastes. When the time had come for Harold to wed, he unquestioningly accepted that it would be an arranged match. As if to encourage compliance and ward off any lingering doubts, the sum of £500 was settled on Harold by his father on the day of the wedding itself, a substantial amount early this century.

But where to find a wife with whom this fortune and future could be shared? It was a timely opportunity for the intervention of 'Uncle Bob'. He had contacts with the Mandel family in Germany and it was considered that Bertha Mandel might be a suitable candidate. Bertha was born in eastern Poland, but had moved to Fürth, in Bavaria, at three years of age. Harold Preger and Bertha Mandel exchanged letters, and then photographs. A meeting was arranged; a second followed. But since neither spoke the other's language they were obliged to converse in Yiddish. However, Harold Preger was resourceful enough to woo Bertha with a series of Yiddish songs – and most particularly with the well-known love song '*Shayn vi di Levona*' ('Beautiful is the moon'). When Harold and Bertha met for the third time it was under the *chuppa* (wedding canopy).

For Bertha Mandel it was indeed a good match, for in 1934 the Pregers moved from Waterloo Road to a much more prosperous area. For Manchester Jewry something quite unprecedented had happened: two of its members had moved to premises known not by number but by name. The Pregers' new abode was called The Danes and situated in the much sought-after Crumpsall Lane. Bertha Preger had hardly finished furnishing the house when a dream came true, for it was there that she gave birth to a long-awaited daughter, Anita. Many years later, Anita would recall:

> Crumpsall Lane was more than posh – it was really something quite special. It had just under one acre of land – stables, drawing rooms, polished floors. In fact my parents were the only Jewish family in the entire area at that time.

She was right. The Danes was indeed a select address, and had a garage that could accommodate half a dozen vehicles. The garage was so big that when, five years later, war broke out, it was requisitioned by the National Fire Service. There was even a billiards room. And Bertha's lot was eased considerably by the presence of Annie, a live-in maid from Ireland. A full-time gardener tended to the Pregers' not inconsiderable plot of land. Bertha and Harold had every reason to feel proud: few other Mancunian Jews boasted such an impressive home.

But despite the desirable setting, the Preger household was far from happy. Harold Preger had a strong temper that could on occasion be violent, frequently obliging Bertha to try to restrain him. It was a temper that would in time tax his health quite considerably. Leslie and Jack would regularly receive a *schmeis*, a good clip round the ear. Nor was there any discrimination on the grounds of sex, for Anita would in due course receive her fair share of backhanders too.

Leslie remembers that:

There was not a happy atmosphere at The Danes, at least not by today's standards. There would be no shortage of wallops, sometimes for no apparent reason. My father would also take a strap to our bottoms. The home was quite authoritarian, but it was part of the accepted system of the time. I have to say, though, that materially we were well looked after, and certainly a great priority was given to education.

The Pregers may have moved away from the heart of Manchester's Jewish community, but they retained much of the ghetto mentality. Seldom was there any contact with non-Jews – even the boys' cub-scouts pack was Jewish – and the atmosphere at home remained deeply orthodox. There would be no switching on of lights during the Sabbath. The laws of the *kashrut* were likewise rigorously adhered to, milk and meat being kept separately, as Jews have done since time immemorial. During the festival of Passover these rituals would be adhered to even more strictly. Dishes and glasses were soaked in the bath for three consecutive days before they were deemed sufficiently pure according to the ancient dietary laws. On the eve of Passover, Harold Preger would busy himself sweeping around the corners of the house, and the *khometz* (items not sanctified for Passover) would be burnt the next day. Obsessive cleaning would take place. Indeed, there was so much frenzied scrubbing, wiping and polishing during that particular religious festival that Annie the housekeeper developed an uncanny knack of disappearing to the local pub rather than face the awesome work-load.

The food the Pregers ate was from a tradition spanning several centuries, and of the old heavy Jewish variety. On High Holy days the menu would be repeated time and again: egg and onion or chopped liver as an hors-d'oeuvre, followed by chicken soup served with *kneidlach*, a main course consisting of roast chicken served with a generous assortment of vegetables, followed by *lokschen* pudding. And all of this was washed down, if possible, with a glass of Russian tea. Every single aspect of their lives, from *kashrut* to commerce, was guided, influenced or affected by the dictates of Jewishness. Harold Preger would always ensure that his shops were closed by the appointed hour, so that he could herald the arrival of the Sabbath. And on all of the major fesivals in the Jewish calendar, the entire family would attend the nearest synagogue at High Crumpsall, which followed orthodox rather than reform precepts of Judaism. Anita Preger recalls the atmosphere at home:

Although Annie was from the deepest bogs of Ireland, she soon acquired a good working knowledge of Yiddish. She came to my parents just one month after they were married, so mother and Annie developed a method of communication intelligible only to them. Since mother's English was not very good, I remember she once sent Annie out to buy 'tomorrow's bread', by which I assume she meant a fresh loaf, but when Annie delivered the request literally she succeeded only in confusing the local baker.

Every Friday night, though, the table would be prepared, the candles lit, the wine sanctified and the benediction undertaken. On Pesach we would sit up until two in the morning. As the youngest, I used to have the honour of reading the four questions from the Haggadah, but I always used to insist that Jack carried out his version which was in Yiddish and Hebrew, not English and Hebrew, because to me this was a thing of great beauty. Thus on *yomtovim* (High Holy days), we would sing into the early hours of the morning. Father especially loved to sing, and particularly so on Shabbat.

Harold Preger was certainly able to meet his family's material needs. But his tireless application to the work that provided these benefits was draining his health. The rheumatic fever he suffered in his late twenties would develop over the following twenty-five years into severe cardiac disease and eventually kill him.

Jack's primary school, Crumpsall Lane Elementary Mixed, provided a reasonable standard of education. It also provided something not on the curriculum: the boy's first taste of anti-Semitism. Since Leslie was already at the school, Jack was afforded some degree of protection. Even so, there were fights in the playground, and frequent taunts and bullying. Unlike many Jewish boys, Jack was tall for his age and so able to defend himself – at least for the most part. But once he saw two older boys from the school seize his brother's hair and set it on fire; just for being a Jew. Since the incident occurred near his home, Jack managed to rouse some local residents, who forced the tormentors to beat a hasty retreat. Leslie's hair was extinguished without much damage to scalp or skin. Nonetheless, it was an incident that badly shook up both boys. Not that Jack was always ready to offer his older brother a helping hand, as Leslie remembers:

At Crumpsall Lane we used to have to pay milk-money: a halfpenny a day, tuppence halfpenny per week. One day the headmaster, Mr Fred Ashworth, summoned me. There was Jackie looking very upset – he'd stolen a halfpenny, a day's milk-money from another boy – and he'd hidden it very cleverly in the lining of his waistcoat pocket. But it had been found. When asked why he had taken this money when he already had some of his own, his reply rather put me in it: 'My brother ordered me to steal it!', he boldly declared.

23

The Preger household was in no sense political. Issues of commerce, religion, and education were uppermost in Harold and Bertha's minds. Yet it was impossible to ignore what was happening in Germany. This was hardly surprising, for two reasons: first, because the Nazis had by now been swept into power; second, and most urgently of all, because Bertha's parents were German nationals who continued to live under Hitler's dictatorship, so blatantly hostile to the Jews. The *Manchester Guardian* had exposed Nazi excesses as early as 1933, at a time when other journals could find little space in their columns. That newspaper therefore served a key role in keeping the Pregers well informed. The following is from an article of 1934. Under the headline THE NAZI TERROR GOES ON – MORE EVIDENCE OF PRISON CRUELTY, the paper reported that:

> For a short time it seemed that the Nazi Terror was diminishing, but, according to information now received by your correspondent, it is at least as bad now as it was six months ago. Only it grows more secret and the methods of ill-treatment more ingenious. The well-known prison in the Columbiastrasse, Berlin, has been referred to repeatedly in the *Manchester Guardian*. It now holds some 400 prisoners who are treated with frightful severity, the Jews among them being marked for special treatment.

Unlike many Jews, both German and British, Bertha Preger knew that she had to act. Nor was her husband to remain idle, as Jack explains:

> My father stayed in England but worked with the Quakers trying to get people in Manchester to sponsor these refugees. In other words, to say that they would employ these persecuted Jews as domestic servants or gardeners, but more often than not he would get a very discouraging response. I can still remember him coming back home, dropping into his chair, and saying 'It's hopeless – nobody's interested in signing these forms to get people out.'

By 1938 Bertha Preger was desperate to rescue her parents from the tyranny of Nazism. There was only one thing to do: she would travel to Bavaria, the very heartland of the Third Reich, to see what she could achieve in person, for an endless flow of paperwork and petitions had produced little result. Returning to Nazi Germany was a risky strategy, but one that Bertha now felt compelled to pursue. Scarcely had she arrived at her home town than she was arrested. Worse still, while she was there the Jews of Fürth were rounded up and made to witness the burning of their synagogue, an act of vandalism becoming an increasingly familiar part of Nazi methods. Bertha Preger was paraded around the village square and only released on producing evidence of British nationality.

Perhaps Jack inherited his mother's sense of determination and her campaigning spirit. For her visit proved to be successful, at least in part, because she managed to get her parents back to England. It was a remarkable feat. An article commending Bertha's daring appeared in the *Manchester Guardian*, filling Bertha with justifiable pride. The elderly Mandels settled near Manchester, in Wellington Street, Salford, where many other ultra-orthodox immigrant Jews had chosen to make their homes. However, Bertha's sister and brother-in-law did not escape the net of Nazism; nor was she able to save her brother Shank, who attempted for some time to hide in Poland. Many relatives, cousins and friends were to perish over the next six years. Of course Jack, only eight at the time, did not understand his mother's missions, or what her frequent absences abroad signified. But the message most certainly entered his mind that members of his immediate family were suffering because they were Jews and that his mother was particularly distressed.

Shortly after the outbreak of the Second World War, all three Preger children were evacuated to the villages and farms of Lancashire. In December 1939 Jack was dispatched to the Greenhauch family, whose home was in Mellor, near Blackburn. Was it not a highly traumatic experience to be sent away so suddenly from family and friends? Not for Jack.

No. I loved it. That's when I really got farming into my blood. I just couldn't stop after that because I loved everything about it;

the open air, the scenery, the animals, mixing cattle-cake and so on. This love of farming and the countryside has stayed with me ever since.

Were the Greenhauches sensitive to the requirements, dietary and otherwise, of this young orthodox Jew from the teeming metropolis of Manchester?

Not at all. I still remember the first time I smelled pork. It hit me virtually as soon as I walked in. It became a great joke with the Greenhauches because it was war time and they used to kill a pig illegally and they would have to cure the bacon. We used to take these black-market pigs in the boot of their old Austin to different farms. It was terrible for me. On one occasion the children got hold of some pork and stuffed it into my mouth as a kind of initiation ceremony. What I remember most was the smell. I knew that this was a forbidden food; it was like committing some very serious offence, some sort of sin. But in fact the family were on the whole very kind to me because there was a lot of anti-Semitism in the school which they shielded me from as much as possible.

With Jack helping to cure bacon and sell joints of ham, it was clear that he was drifting away from the more orthodox precepts of Judaism. Although they were aware that their son was becoming increasingly alienated from *Yiddishkeit*, or Jewishness, there was little that Harold and Bertha Preger could do. Unable and unwilling to dictate a list of demands to the Greenhauches, they were obliged to settle for a rather unsatisfactory compromise. This was periodically to dispatch a reverend from Manchester to keep Jack in touch with the Jewish way of life. The Pregers were too proud of their heritage to let it lapse so easily.

After some eight months with the Greenhauches, Jack moved to a second family — the Halliwells, who lived at Sykes Farm in Coxted Green. When the itinerant reverend eventually tracked Jack down at this somewhat remote address, he was quick to ask about his diet. To his horror, he would receive an answer such as:

'A special treat today, Reverend. The farmer's wife prepared a packed lunch for me today and I took it to school. It was crab sandwich – delicious.'

The reverend would then scuttle back to Manchester and report to Jack's parents the extent to which their son had strayed from even the most elementary teachings of the Talmud. Unless something was done at once, he warned them, Jack might well be lost to Judaism for all time. There was no question about it: crabs and the *kashrut* simply did not mix. Bertha and Harold Preger were left to ponder on the most satisfactory course of action.

By 1941 Jack had won a place at Stand Grammar, a school originally founded in 1688 and serving the Prestwich, Radcliffe and Whitefield areas of Manchester. It was said that Robert Clive – Clive of India – had been a pupil there in the eighteenth century and a plaque bearing his name was prominently and proudly displayed. It was a gentle reminder to parents and pupils alike that there was no reason why the current intake should not leave their mark on the world. However, Clive's attendance at the school might be pure legend, since a thorough attempt by one headmaster to find hard evidence of it ended in failure, although a letter referring to his enrolment was displayed at the school shortly after the turn of the century. Whatever the truth, 'It had nothing whatsoever to do with my coming out to Calcutta,' insists Preger.

Young Jack's interest was rooted firmly in matters Spanish, not Indian. The origins of this early attraction to Spanish culture and language were by no means difficult to detect: they were directly attributable to his enduring hero-worship of his father's brother, Lazzy. Uncle Lazzy had been a committed communist from his youth. Not only had he been to the Soviet Union, he was also the first communist from the north of England to volunteer to fight with the International Brigade in the Spanish civil war. While working as an ambulance driver in Spain, he went out of his way to supply his young nephew with postage stamps for his collection, and would tell the boy in very great detail about his wartime experiences. Jack was extremely proud of his Uncle Lazzy and this pride would later ignite in him not just a passion for the Spanish language and literature, but a sympathy for and attraction to left-wing politics in general. These were early influences on the boy, and all the more powerful for that.

Jack's thirst for all things Spanish was carefully developed and encouraged by the school's very able Spanish teacher, Mr Hawley, who nurtured the boy's enthusiasm for that country so skilfully that learning its language became a pleasure rather than a chore. Hawley's approach was not at all academic, for having worked and travelled extensively in Latin America he simply built on his experiences there. Jack was in no doubt: he was hungry to learn more.

In the interwar years, for every boy entering medicine, veterinary science and dentistry, at least eight went to work in the mills and factories of the industrial north. Leslie Preger, then also a Stand Grammar boy, would later concede that his younger brother was 'much the brighter boy at school – very much a gifted child'. And unlike their earlier experiences at Crumpsall Lane, there was a conspicuous absence of anti-Semitism at the school. For Jack and Leslie alike, they were happy days at Stand Grammar.

The evenings, however, were quite unlike those spent by most of their contemporaries. For as Jack embarked upon preparations for his Barmitzvah, he became a student at the Manchester Yeshiva, and fell under the influence of the Reverend Jonas Bolkein, who had a reputation for his meticulous and disciplined approach to religious study. Although unaware of it at the time, Jack was about to enter a religious phase that would last until his mid-teens. As he now recalls:

> I became extremely religious whereas my brother remained fairly sane. I was an average student at the Yeshiva but gradually I worked harder and became very interested in Hebrew studies, so much so in fact that they began to say, 'He's got the makings of a rabbi, you know, that boy.'

Nor did the young Yeshiva student's devotion to his studies go unnoticed by fellow pupils, who wasted no time in dubbing him a future rabbi. It might well have been a joke, but there was an element of truth in it. Witnessing his younger brother adhere increasingly to the more orthodox precepts of Judaism was strange for Leslie. Nevertheless, Jack was by no means unusual:

There were a lot of *frummers* [ultra-orthodox Jews] around then, so it didn't strike me as all that extraordinary. My parents were quite pleased, although at times it was quite inconvenient having someone so religious in the house. I remember my father used to be quite embarrassed to smoke in front of Jackie on Shabbat, even though he was still a lad barely coming up for his Barmitzvah.

Developing a love of the Hebrew language, prayers and melodies, Jack took his new found faith seriously. On one occasion, during the festival of Tish B'av, Jack was so profoundly moved by the story of the destruction of the Temple in Jerusalem that he prostrated himself and cried out loud, such was his grief at the suffering inflicted on his forebears. When, in 1943, Jack's Barmitzvah took place at a synagogue in Hightown, his recital of the portion of the law was as perfect as anyone could recall.

Jack had indeed become deeply religious, but that did not mean that he could not occasionally cause trouble for those more spiritually advanced than him. As Leslie recalls:

During these war years there was a small local synagogue called Fox's *shul*, which was in a converted house, and it was always particularly difficult to get a *minyan* [a quorum for prayer] on a weekday, so it was decided to pay *minyan*-men. Jackie and I and another friend called Asher Wolfish went there early in the morning. After some time Asher called a strike in order to effect a small pay increase, and this was successful. I remember that this infuriated my grandfather — not long out of Nazi Germany — who thought that making up a *minyan* should be something approaching a *mitzvah* [pleasure].

Three years after his Barmitzvah Jack's religious phase had run its course. But why?

29

I think I was growing up. I was walking along on my way home from school one day when I decided to take my *yarmulka* off – an unknown thing for an orthodox Jew then to walk along bareheaded. It was an incredible sensation to feel the breeze in my hair. I told my mother that I was not going to the Yeshiva that night, pretending I had too much homework. It wasn't anything dramatic. My faith just went down the drain. I just didn't believe in any of it any more. I had been kept in this kind of box of orthodox Judaism. Your whole life was work and study and worship and going to *shul*. You came home from school, had your tea, then you went to the Yeshiva. Came home from the Yeshiva, then you would start your homework. It was a terrible burden. I couldn't play soccer at school because the teams played on Shabbat. So once I took my *yarmulka* off I experienced this really tremendous sense of liberation. I felt, I'm alive now. In any event there were always things that never made any sense to me. Like I'd been on the farm with *goyim*, and I knew that they were human beings – contrary to many of the messages I had been receiving elsewhere. The Greenhauches had been extremely kind to me, but that was never accepted by Jews in those days – all *goyim* were seen as a kind of inferior being. I had had enough of the lot of it.

It was another sixteen years before any religious convictions re-appeared. They were, though, at a considerable remove from this discarded Jewish faith. Free now from the constraints of the Yeshiva, Jack was left with much more time to apply himself to secular studies. Few of the teachers harboured any doubts about Jack's ability: he was unquestionably the brightest boy in the school. There was really only one place suitable for the completion of this promising academic career: Oxford. Jack took English literature, Spanish and Geography for his higher certificates, the first forming the core of his preparatory work for the Oxford entrance examinations.

Being a serious student did not mean that Jack had acquired the knack of cutting himself off from the real world. On the contrary, there were times when his compassion would make quite an impact on others; on his sister Anita, for example:

> Jack has always had a strong sympathy with the underdog. I remember once during a Jewish festival there was a sermon, and all the kids would gather outside to socialize. Of course it was also an occasion for the boys and girls to see who had eyes for who. My brother was always tall and good-looking – in fact I think it was during the Yiskor ceremony, the part when the kids go out and the dead are remembered, yet he went out of his way to go up and speak to this girl who was particularly plain. She was also partly paralysed and used a stick – she always appeared to be left out and on her own. Yet Jack went over and spent some time chatting and getting to know her. He was only about fourteen then and I remember thinking how nice this was.

Jack could also be mischevious. There were the traditional and time-honoured acts of defiance, like smoking black Sobranie tobacco in the toilets of Stand Grammar with his friend Henry Livings. Sometimes he would get away with defying the authorities. And sometimes not, as Anita remembers:

> Jack once met a non-Jewish girl who lived further along Crumpsall Lane. He must have been about fifteen at that time. She rang the door bell on Shabbat afternoon – itself quite rare. She disturbed my mother smoking, which mother should not have been doing, although her self-imposed discipline was never to smoke in front of the candles! The girl came in and mother and I and the girl sat and sat and sat – we hadn't met her before. Eventually she enquired, 'Is Jack home?' At six o'clock she left. Jack returned an hour later, and got hell as soon as he walked through the door. She must have latched on to him. He felt sorry for her, and invited her to tea, but decided not to turn up. Typical of Jack, that, full of practical jokes.

Jack might have dispensed with the practice of orthodox Judaism, but his Jewishness was not to be stifled quite so easily. As the

31

religious side of Judaism was quietly abandoned, so its politics came to the fore. It was hardly a surprising turn of events, for Jack had spent the greater part of the war at home with his mother who, throughout that period, had continued to involve herself with the plight of refugees from Germany. Her efforts had met with some success; she had, after all, got her own parents out of Nazi Germany. But many cousins, relatives and friends had perished in what Nazi ideology referred to as the Final Solution to the Jewish problem. As the end of the war approached, and the downfall of the Third Reich became inevitable, Bertha Preger contributed considerable time and money towards the purchase of a house intended for children whose parents had been slaughtered in the Holocaust.

Now seventeen, Jack was convinced that this time he had got it right: in order to prevent a repetition of the atrocities inflicted on European Jewry, there now had to be a homeland for the Jews. It was a matter of the utmost urgency. Launching himself into the world of Zionist youth, a new and highly politicized Yaacob Preger – for that was his real first name – had arrived.

The forum for this newly embraced political creed was a Zionist organization called Hashomer Hatzair (Young Watchman), a left-wing group who believed that the economy of any future Jewish homeland should be both planned and controlled centrally. Wealth should be distributed equally among the people. It was perhaps a natural response to Fascism, and one that Jack readily endorsed. His father, however, did not share his enthusiasm for the partition of Palestine. And Harold Preger was equally unenthusiastic about the concept of *Aliyah* (Jewish emigration to Palestine), particularly for his son. In fact when Jack went on a long-awaited visit to Spain in 1948, he was obliged to promise his father, with a solemn oath and undertaking, that he would in no circumstances take a trip to Marseilles, from where boats were regularly setting out for (and being turned back from) the Promised Land.

Zionism, then unpopular with the greater part of British Jewry, was in the air. For Jack Preger, so too was love. Having stayed on at Stand Grammar to sit for the Oxford entrance examinations, he moved from Manchester to Bedfordshire, where Hashomer Hatzair's training kibbutz was situated. The idea was to give those

intent on making *Aliyah* the flavour of agricultural life in prep-
aration for their departure to the fledgling Zionist state. Many of
those on the camp were 'DPs' – displaced persons from Europe
whose families had been brutalized by the Nazis. The kibbutz was
in reality a smallholding attached to a large house on the Cambridge
Road just outside of Bedford. There was within the grounds a metal
workshop, but one of Jack's tasks was to go out and earn money for
the kibbutz by working for a building contractor as a labourer.
Although from a prosperous family and about to pursue an academic career at Oxford, Jack had never been afraid to get his hands
dirty.

It was on an outing organized by the kibbutz that Jack met
Annette Zweig. As they travelled down to Swiss Cottage in London
to attend a concert, the atmosphere was an exciting mixture of fun
and idealism. Sitting in the back of the kibbutz's lorry on his way to
the concert, Jack sang Zionist songs, Hebrew melodies and of
course the Hatikvah. Annette was active in the London branch of
Hashomer Hatzair and from a middle-class family from Stamford
Hill, north-east London, where her father worked as a furrier. Jack
and Annette fell in love. Like Jack, Annette was undecided whether
or not to go on *Aliyah*.

By 1948 the State of Israel had not only been declared, it was
fighting for its very survival against a formidable array of Arab
armies attacking on several fronts. From Hashomer Hatzair's
perspective, it was simply not good enough to be lukewarm about
the prospect of making *Aliyah*. You either did it or you did not.
Most of its members did it willingly. Jack Preger did not.

I was on the kibbutz between school and national service. It was
in 1948, and they said to me, 'We're all going on *Aliyah* – you
come with us.' They also said that I wouldn't be able to go into
the British Army or to university. It was not that I was opposed to
going to Israel and working on a kibbutz, because I did feel that
being a kibbutznik might be the way of life most suited to me – I
had got farming into my blood during my evacuation. I had
certainly become unable to relate very closely to life within the
Manchester Jewish community. But by then I had won a place at

33

Oxford, which had been a lot of hard graft, obliging me to take a special credit in Latin which was a requirement in those days — and I just wasn't willing to give it up that easily. My call-up had been delayed, so I wouldn't have minded skipping the army, but it was on the issue of not taking up my place at Oxford that Hashomer Hatzair and I parted ways.

There were many occasions over the next two years, during which time he dutifully carried out his national service, when Jack had reason to wish that he had left for the Holy Land after all. For he experienced a brand of anti-Semitism that made his earlier experiences at Crumpsall Lane seem positively tame. For example, on a course organized by the Educational Corps there was a Colonel Commandant who exhorted his conscripts to: 'Remember, gentlemen, that at all times you should let Christianity be the sheet-anchor of your lives.' It was a message singularly inappropriate for the mixed-religion audience before him.

In the barrack room it was total persecution. There was an uninterrupted flow of jibes and taunts, none of them original, and most exhorting Preger to 'go back to your own country'. There was also a barrage of the already familiar slang referring to the Jews, 'yid', 'kike' and 'sheeny' being among the most popular terms of abuse. For Jack, well informed about the plight of European Jewry because of his own family's experience, it was a particularly harrowing time. He found it difficult to comprehend how naked anti-Semitism could remain so rampant when the truth about the concentration camps of Auschwitz and Belsen was still emerging. There was just one escape: regular weekend visits to Annette and her family in Stamford Hill.

There was in fact another, equally reliable, safety-valve: Jack's sense of humour. On one occasion all the young conscripts were particularly anxious for their next leave. Jack managed to obtain a piece of official paper, on which he wrote, in his most bureaucratic hand, the worst message imaginable:

'All leave cancelled forthwith and until further notice.'

There was uproar in the ranks, the majority of the young soldiers simply refusing to perform the duties required of them. It was a typical Preger prank, but Jack's superior officer succeeded in extracting a full confession:

'And are you aware, Preger, of the penalty for officers who cause a mutiny.'

'No, Sir.'

'Death!' thundered the commanding officer.

In the event, the consequences were rather less far-reaching, for Jack was simply demoted. Bertha Preger was rather upset, being unused to seeing her son going down the ladder rather than up it. But for Jack it proved to be a rather good move, for after that incident he enjoyed national service considerably more.

Besides, there had always been Oxford to sustain him throughout the year and a half of duty to King and Country. Jack had won a place to read PPE (philosophy, politics and economics) at St Edmund Hall and the thought of returning to an academic environment, well removed from Manchester and the army, filled him with enthusiasm.

By the autumn of 1950, when Jack was about to go up to Oxford, Harold Preger's health was failing. The business that he had so carefully cultivated was likewise in decline, with little money remaining to meet the considerable expenses of the family home. Still, the Pregers had every reason to be proud of their two boys. Leslie was well on his way to qualifying as a doctor and Jack had gained an exhibition to study at Oxford University, the foremost academic institution in the land.

Shortly before Jack was due to register at St Edmund Hall, the *Rosh*, the head of the Manchester Yeshiva, approached Harold Preger. He had not forgotten the promising young student who he had hoped might one day become a rabbi. Time then for one last attempt to bring the lapsed boy back into the fold. 'How on earth can you,' the bearded *Rosh* challenged them, 'allow your son to go to Yoxford?' (The *Rosh* was playing on the word '*yok*', the most derogatory term in Yiddish for a gentile.) When Jack learned of this incident he treated the question with all the contempt it deserved. He would be going to Oxford, come hell or high water.

3
Teddy Hall

Jack Preger had been desperate to get into Oxford, but it had proved exceedingly difficult to gain a place. He therefore had reason to be doubly proud, for he had won an exhibition, or scholarship, to St Edmund Hall, and such munificence was certainly not common. Latin had been studied as an additional subject, examinations and interviews completed, national service loyally carried out, Zionism abandoned. Jack had a single-mindedness that had impressed a good many people, particularly his parents. And all for this one precise purpose: to complete his education at an institution universally acknowledged as the best. For almost half a millenium nearly every able mind in the country had dreamed of a place at Oxford. Yet within weeks of arriving at St Edmund Hall, Jack was as desperate to get out as he had been to get in. What happened during that first term to produce such an abrupt and fundamental about-turn? Was 'Teddy Hall' not as cosy as its affectionate nickname implied?

The Halls of Oxford had been the original homes of the more junior members of the university, although one by one they had been swallowed up by the richer colleges. St Edmund Hall somehow survived that process and remains justifiably proud of its status as Oxford's last surviving medieval hall. When Preger was there, from 1950 to 1953, life in Hall was full of ritual, with grace being recited in Latin by the Principal or his deputy. Dinner was always served

36

and it was usually preceded by drinks in the Buttery or by darts in the Eastgate pub, then a small and intimate drinking-house. Bach's Toccata and Fugue in D would often reverberate out of the chapel and across the ancient quad. For those fresh from the best of England's public schools, it was a deeply familiar atmosphere, almost home from home. For Jack Preger, however, who six years earlier was one of the more devout students of the Manchester Yeshiva, it was almost as if he had landed on a deeply alien and manifestly hostile planet. Full of divinity students and run by Church of England ministers, the college had only one Jew — Preger.

I felt as if my accent was wrong. My background was certainly wrong. And my religion was wrong. Oxford was very much a public-school place. And although I had completed national service, even that was regarded as fairly bizarre. Because I had fallen foul of the Education Corps after that incident concerning the cancellation of all leave, I ended up in the ranks as a private soldier, whereas virtually everyone else had been commissioned.

St Edmund Hall had established a formidable reputation for excellence in all aspects of sport. When the Dean addressed the new term's Freshmen in the Old Dining Room, he had not minced his words:

'In the sporting world we are the "tops". Academically? Well, what can I say?'

It was true. Academic high-flyers had always steered clear of Teddy Hall, while those with sporting prowess could not get there quickly enough. But whereas Jack's contemporaries such as Robert Lunn would go on to play soccer for England, or distinguish themselves in rugby and cricket, Jack himself did not excel in any sport. True, he would in time represent Oxford at cross-country running in a contest against London University, but only to tie for last place.

Full of sophisticates, St Edmund Hall appeared to be a place where everybody was somebody. Jack Preger was in no doubt: not only was he a nobody, he was a northerner, a grammar-school boy, a Jew whose parents had made good, the eternal outsider.

News from Manchester hardly helped. Harold Preger had become seriously ill. Although only in his fifties, Jack's father had proved unable to fight off persistent cardiac disease, and now it was uncertain how much longer he would live. Some said a matter of years, others that it was more likely only a few months. But no one thought that it would be very long.

Jack sank into a depression. It was not merely a case of being down in the dumps, that feeling of despondency that many experience from time to time. Jack showed virtually every symptom of clinical depression, an altogether more serious disorder, as he would later realize:

I had sleeping difficulties, early morning wakening, loss of appetite, and loss of concentration. I became irritable, withdrawn, had problems with my work, problems with keeping in touch with friends who were up at university, and problems with making contact with new people.

Unaware at the time that he was suffering from a mental disorder, Preger was concerned above all else to leave Oxford as rapidly as possible. His analysis was reasonable enough: everything had been perfectly all right before stepping into the new and bizarre environment of St Edmund Hall. Now, loathing Oxford and everything it represented, he felt the only logical thing to do was to pull out before things got even worse.

His mind was made up. Having booked an appointment to see the Dean of St Edmund Hall, John McManners, Preger planned to ask to be allowed to 'go down' for a year. Since the Dean doubled as a tutor in politics, he had already had some contact with Preger. Certainly he was aware of his student's Jewish faith, for Preger had never sought to disguise it. In fact Jack was about to receive a good deal more than he bargained for.

Preger spoke from the heart as he related to the Dean a tale of insurmountable woes:

I really cannot stand this place any more. I would like to be allowed to go down for a year, to give myself time to think. My father is ill and I don't know when he is going to die. I really don't know if I am going to be able to continue at Oxford or not. I think the best thing to do is for me to have some time off.

McManners was more than sympathetic. He offered sound and practical advice, telling Jack that he should try to put his worries into separate compartments and work on each one of them individually. It was the sort of counsel with which Uncle Lazzy, or indeed Jack's own father, would no doubt have heartily concurred. But then the Dean added something that, to Preger, was quite startling. In time it would be part of a process that would change his entire life.

There is one other thing I should say. You know my religion. I am a Christian. And as a Christian I would not hesitate to turn to Christ for comfort in such a situation. I have to tell you of Christ because Christ is my belief. And for me I know that Christ would be the source of enormous comfort.

It was not an attempt at conversion; far from it. It was merely a statement of belief, the Dean's personal credo. For Jack, however, it was an earth-shattering revelation. He had never heard anything like it in his life:

As he was talking to me I really felt something, a real kind of peace, for the first time in ages. I didn't start reading the Bible or anything like that, and it didn't make me a Christian, but I've never forgotten the sensation I felt then – that there is some calmness, some peace here – and he gave me enough hope to go out and cope with all this. I resolved to try to stick it out in this crazy place, this very posh college, this incredible university. So the Dean's words to me did point to something of real value. And I know I'm not making all of this up retrospectively because of the profound shock I felt when McManners spoke of Jesus. It was all done in a couple of minutes or so, but something was most definitely placed in my mind then.

As for the depression, the Dean's talk most certainly did the trick. Or rather it did for the moment, for mental disorders have a habit of haunting those who suffer from them, as Jack would in time discover.

Jack's sense of isolation had not been without foundation. Although no longer a practising Jew and now firmly agnostic, he readily embraced logical positivism, then the most fashionable philosophical concept at Oxford. Yet Jack retained the belief that somehow he did not belong. For whereas Robert Lunn could report that:

. . . another of my special joys was the Sunday service. A time for quiet thought and reflection in this intimate and peaceful chapel following each busy week. A good solid down-to-earth service, well led with well-known hymns and prayers. I always emerged revitalized . . . ,

of course Preger did not emerge at all, being the only person from the entire Hall not to attend the service. Unlike in the army, where anti-Semitism had been both blatant and ferocious, at Oxford a new and more discreet sensation was encountered. It manifested itself in a series of unseen and unspoken undercurrents:

The feeling was that 'you are certainly not one of us' – a veiled kind of anti-Semitism which was entirely new to me. On the other hand, if you were outstanding at some kind of sport, or absolutely brilliant, or if you were some kind of a character – then these kind of things could establish you in spite of being Jewish.

Without realizing it, Jack had hit on a new strategy. While he might well have been among the brightest and best at Stand Grammar, at the University of Oxford, long used to creaming off the best minds of Britain, he was confronted by the fact that he was no longer top of the class. Nor was he a champion sportsman, on a par with Lunn and his friends. In Preger's mind, there was only one option: to become 'some kind of a character'. It was still to take some time, but by the end of his second year at Oxford, Jack had firmly established himself as an active member of what he would later describe as the 'Oxford lunatic fringe'. Apparently, a Jewish lunatic from the north of England was eminently acceptable.

Preger never sought to be rid of his Jewish roots. In any event, there would have been little chance of a successful eradication. For there was always Uncle Lazzy, hero of the Spanish civil war, to remind Jack of his Ashkenazi stock. Periodically he would send postcards to his nephew, each laced with a delightful blend of humour and Yiddish. Oxford might well be the city of 'dreaming spires' in innumerable tourist guides, but such literature evidently did not feature on Uncle Lazzy's reading list. Lazzy's postcard messages were always a good deal more succinct:

> Dear Jackie,
> I hope you are enjoying the *verschloofinah* [slumbering] spires!
> Love from Uncle Lazzy.

In 1953 another Jew, David Goldstein, arrived at St Edmund Hall. Jack had little contact with him. But Goldstein also had reason to turn to the Dean. Although his troubles were of a more practical nature, once again the Dean's approach was more than sympathetic, as Goldstein later recalled:

> I was in desperate need of a subfusc suit for Matriculation. My grant money had not yet arrived. So I turned to the Dean, John McManners. His clerical collar made me worry. I thought he might try to convert a poor Jewish boy like me. I had heard of such things. But he was understanding, simple, straightforward and sympathetic. He also gave me the money. . . .

Jack was no longer engaged in battle with Oxford. Peace had broken out at St Edmund Hall. McManners was especially vigilant, constantly keeping a benevolent eye on the student he had reassured so effectively. Jack was having a good time and, significantly, enjoying the philosophy, politics and economics that he was there to study. Staircase number four had become quite fun. There was a particularly able tutor in economics, Professor Allen, who provoked and stimulated Jack in long and challenging individual tutorials, which on occasion lasted a good three hours. Allen went out of his way to introduce Preger to Asa Briggs, who was not a public figure during the 1950s, but whose teaching of social economic history seldom failed to inspire and delight. Unknown to Preger, Briggs's analysis of the conditions in the workhouses of Victorian England would be dusted down and used again almost a quarter of a century later.

Professor Allen had immersed himself in a subject that had struggled hard to find its way on to the academic syllabus: the agricultural economics of underdeveloped countries. It was a subject in which Jack found himself particularly at home, mainly because a love of the land and of all things agricultural had always remained very close to his heart. His carefree days in the country with the Greenhauches during the evacuation, had firmly lodged themselves in Jack's memory.

So comfortable was he with this new subject that Jack decided to take it as a special paper. His essay 'The Economic Development of Underdeveloped Countries' might not form part of the standard reading on the subject, but it was a piece of research and writing to which he applied himself with remarkable energy and enthusiasm. But then he had good reason to do so. Allen had dangled before his eyes a carrot that might prove to be very tasty indeed: the possibility of a job as a research assistant in Ghana, West Africa. There was only one snag: to get to Ghana, Preger would need to obtain nothing less than a first-class degree. In the event, it was some years before he set out to work in the Third World and his first port of call was in Asia rather than Africa.

Even while at Oxford Jack found himself unable to stay away from tilling the land. Farming was still in his blood. Whereas his contemporaries sought early experience in the City, or attempted to acquire practical knowledge in law or medicine, Jack was constantly heading off to a local farm, determined to get his hands dirty. Nor was it easy to secure work on a farm. One farmer's wife was particularly suspicious of Jack's motives and credentials. She even telephoned the Vice Principal of St Edmund Hall, to test Jack's unlikely story and to ask, if it were true, for a reference. As the Vice Principal happened to be Jack's tutor in moral philosophy, he was well aware of his student's potential.

'Yes,' he replied without the slightest hesitation, 'I think that's broadly within his competence.' So Jack became surely the best-educated part-time farm labourer in the whole of Oxfordshire.

In 1952, after a long illness, Harold Preger died. He was only fifty-five years of age. Since his father's death was not at all unexpected, Jack had prepared himself for it and had in a way embarked in advance on a period of mourning. The Dean of St Edmund Hall, so helpful two years earlier, was again at hand with comfort and support. Bertha, however, was by no means as well prepared as her son. Although secure financially, she was devastated by early widowhood and entered a long and slow decline, above all psychologically.

It was during Jack's Oxford years that the romance with Annette Zweig disintegrated. Now that they were far from their common domain of Hashomer Hatzair, it came as no surprise to either that the relationship did not last. There were visits on a number of occasions, but love seemed to evaporate almost as quickly as it had sprung up. At Oxford during the early fifties male students outnumbered females by some seven to one. Not that Jack had any difficulty in attracting members of the opposite sex. Tall, fair-haired, good-looking and fit, he had a regular flow of girlfriends, some of them nurses, who were always much in demand among undergraduates. Had Bertha known that the majority of these girls were not Jewish, she would no doubt have been horrified, but Jack made a conscious effort not to broadcast the ethnic origins of his female companions.

But what of Oxford's lunatic fringe? There was really no doubt about it: Jack Preger was an eminently suitable candidate for full membership. Already in his second year at Oxford he had struck up a great friendship with John Justice, whose background was distinctly upper-class and continental, and with a young woman named Serena Wadham, a recent convert to Catholicism who lived at Donnington Manor. Although in later years Preger would have a different attitude to Catholicism, here was, for the moment at least, too good an opportunity to miss. Wearing hired Roman Catholic priests' robes, Preger and Justice set off to put Serena's new-found faith to the test. On arriving at Donnington Manor they were scarcely able to conceal repeated bouts of convulsive giggling that threatened to wreck the entire mission. A bemused maid courteously enquired:

'And who shall I say called?'

'Fathers Murphy and Jones' – the best names the two students were able to muster.

However, as Serena and her parents were out, the episode served only as a dress rehearsal for later stunts.

Returning thwarted to the station for their train back to Oxford, the 'Fathers' managed to hitch a lift from a kindly driver, who asked innocently enough:

'Must you really wear a collar on a wonderful day like today?'

Preger was in his element, and there was no stopping him now. The Jew had been accepted. There was no disputing the fact that Jack Preger had become known as a character. Boosted by the daring of their excursion to Donnington Manor, Preger and Justice were now all the time assuming various disguises, and constantly scanning the terrain for new objects worthy of ridicule. The purpose of these carefully planned excursions? Most usually to shock, or startle – anything to produce a dramatic reaction. The criterion was simple: almost any stunt was worth trying as long as it made life more entertaining.

They once planned to make an appearance as Flemish dockers, but eventually setled for a hoax at the expense of the Oxford University Jewish Society. As a former student of the Manchester Yeshiva, Preger was particularly well equipped to organize and choreograph the entire jape. He first informed the Jewish Society that a *Gallach* was coming up from London. Preger had come to convey the message: the Jewish holy man would be more than happy to be the Society's guest speaker.

This time the roles were to be reversed, for Jack's non-Jewish fellow-conspirator was to play the rabbi. The theatrical costumiers, who had had no difficulty in attiring bogus Catholic priests, were quite unable to do likewise for their Jewish counterparts. Preger, Justice and the other plotters were forced to settle for a home-made version, but one benefit of this was that no additional expenditure was incurred. Their improvised get-up of beards and black robes must surely have been effective. For the '*goishe Gallach*', as he came to be known, conducted a rather lengthy interview for the university newspaper, in which he held forth on a wide range of matters spiritual. And the ranking on the Preger-Justice scale of mischief? A resounding success – and confirmation of their belief that careful planning was the secret.

Jack was on a high. Delighted not to have abandoned Oxford precipitately during that troubled first term, he had apparently not only seen off his depression, he had knocked it for six. Or had he? This cycle – up one moment and down the next – is a familiar part of a mental disorder known as manic-depressive psychosis. Was Jack suffering from this illness while he was at Oxford? Most probably he was, but it was only in much later life that he would describe himself in this way. Certainly his behaviour as a student demonstrated all the classic symptoms. Jack had become rather like the Grand Old Duke of York – when he was up he was up, and when he was down he was down. But here the similarity ends, for perhaps the most troubling feature of manic-depressive illness is that the sufferer has absolutely no control over or insight into why he is marching in one particular direction as opposed to the other.

When Jack parted company with Hashomer Hatzair he also said goodbye to its passion for Zion, perhaps the principal hallmark of that movement. Yet its fundamentalist, left-wing analysis of economic and social affairs remained deeply attractive. In a world still reeling from the ravages of a war instigated by the expansionary ambitions of nations that had embraced Fascism, Communism appeared to be the ideal antidote. An active member of the Oxford University Socialist Party, Preger became a college representative of the Socialist club, and for anyone harbouring doubts about which way society should be heading, Preger had the ready answer: Marxism, the pathway to the future.

Oxford, although an important part of the British establishment, was also home to a number of leading Marxists, of whom Preger's professor of economics was one. Allen's diagnosis was hardly original, and appeared at times as if it had been lifted directly from Marx's *Das Kapital*, published back in 1867:

> If you look at the oppression of working people under capitalism . . . although gross national product might well increase under this system as it develops, you will notice that the proportionate share going to the workers does not increase, and might well diminish, so that in fact working people, who create this wealth, always tend to end up worse off as the development of capitalism takes place.

It was an analysis that Preger endorsed wholeheartedly. But while the professor dispensed such views, albeit with great conviction, from the relative security of academia, Jack was eager to convert this compelling new theory into practice. And nowhere was the need to do this more pressing than in his beloved Spain. It was in this spirit of reform and revolution that Preger set off with John Justice in the summer of 1952 to visit anti-Franco elements operating clandestinely in that country, passing the odd message of support here and there. It was hardly the work of a full-time revolutionary, but Preger was to become passionately committed to the overthrow of Franco, as his Uncle Lazzy had been before him.

Already the intellectual, Jack steeped himself in music, particularly the playing of Segovia, and spent many hours listening to Sibelius. He devoured the novels of Graham Greene and displayed a similarly healthy appetite for Spanish poetry. Intense, earnest, sincere he might have been, but he also knew how to have fun. Towards the end of one summer term Jack had moved out of St Edmund Hall and into digs run by a particularly stern landlady. For several weeks she steadfastly refused him permission to hold a party. Nor would St Edmund Hall have provided a suitable alternative venue, since no females were allowed to remain in students' rooms after seven p.m. Jack seized on a new strategy. When he anounced his engagement to Serena Wadham, the landlady immediately relented and gave her blessing to the proposed celebrations. Presents for the young couple arrived at her home, which she received on their behalf with genuine pleasure. A first-class party was thrown. It was, of course, another Preger prank, shared by Serena, Justice, the guests and almost everybody but the unsuspecting landlady.

Amid all this frivolity, Jack had little idea of where he was heading. When he was awarded a second-class degree, only one thing was clear to him: that he would not be setting out for Ghana to carry out postgraduate research. And John Justice, for one, could see that his friend was far from settled:

> We were the closest of friends at Oxford, and it has to be said that we really did have more than our fair share of laughs. But I could see quite clearly that there was always a general restlessness with Jack. He always appeared to be searching. Never satisfied, there always appeared to be a sour touch about him.

It was true. Preger was indeed searching. He had abandoned Jewish orthodoxy; Zionism too. The appeal of the left remained strong, but this could hardly form the basis of a career. As it was, Jack embarked on a path that could hardly have been less appropriate:

> I was pushed into something by the university's appointments board. I hadn't done statistics as part of my finals because I knew that mathematically I was pretty hopeless, but they nonetheless concluded that I should go into market research. I followed their advice.

St Edmund Hall has over the years produced a remarkably assorted crop of students: an ambassador, a very senior civil servant, a variety of dons, the proprietor of an Italian restaurant, journalists, a brigadier, an actor, a TV producer, a Bishop of Mashonaland, a West African government official, scientists, parsons and schoolmasters galore. It also produced Jack Preger, trainee market researcher, for Jack was offered a job by a London company, Attwood Statistics Limited. This was a period of employment destined not to last long, for Jack's search for himself was only just beginning.

4

Farming for What?

Jack's new job was hardly challenging. His first task was to test a variety of chocolates and prepare reports on them. When Jack's taste buds were not being artificially stimulated, his nostrils were hard at work sampling the widely differing aromas that emanated from rival perfumes. In addition, there was a constant flow of statistics to juggle with, and then further reports to compile. The young Oxford graduate, smartly but soberly dressed, was allocated a desk in a basement that was particularly ungenerous with its quota of natural daylight. It did not take Jack long to realize that his commitment to market research was not as wholehearted as he had once indicated to his employers.

> I would sit there at that desk and wonder what on earth I was doing. I knew it wasn't for me, and before long I was absolutely loathing going into work. I began to see that miserable little room as a form of imprisonment and knew that I just had to get out.

Jack's liberation came sooner than he had anticipated. For after six months of grappling with graphs, he was abruptly asked to resign. It was an enormous relief to be able to oblige; the nightmare had finally come to an end. But while working for Attwood Statistics, Jack had entered into another commitment, and this would last a good deal longer than his brief flirtation with market research. Her name was Maritta. She remembers:

> It was not love at first sight with Jack. Not at all. I was an art student in digs in Chelsea, and I attended the Chelsea School of Art. There was no electricity in the house — it was lit by gas. The retired nurse who ran the place used to insist that the students be either all boys or all girls — never mixed. She only came to break this rule when she decided to sell the house, and she took in Jack as a lodger.

Maritta's background could scarcely have been more different from Jack's in terms of both religion and culture. Her father was a doctor; her grandfather had been a clergyman in the West Indies. Jack had spent his formative years in the studious atmosphere of the Manchester Yeshiva, while Maritta had grown up in rural Wales, where the Church of England had played a pivotal role in almost all aspects of family life. Even so, when Jack and Maritta began going out together they immediately found an enormous amount of common ground, not least a strong and mutual physical attraction. Both enormously appreciative of the arts, they also shared a particular love of music, films and the theatre.

With his career direction still undecided, Jack took a series of temporary jobs, each connected in some way with matters agricultural. It was a familiar pattern of retreating to the land, but at least this seldom failed to refresh and revitalize him. When John Justice required casual labour on his small gentleman's farm in Devon, Jack was more than happy to help out. He then took a job as a tractor driver for the London Cooperative Society at Turrells Hall, Ongar, in Essex. For Jack there was only one compelling reason to remain in London: the dark-haired Chelsea art student. The relationship flourished, as Maritta explains:

> I went to live in the Fulham Road and Jack would go off relief milking. We got used to being with one another, and enjoyed the same sort of films and music. I missed him enormously when he went away and there would be wonderful reunions on his return

to London. But I did notice, almost from the outset, that Jack would have these extreme swings of mood. Being Church of England, I wanted to know all about Jack's religion and past, but he was always particularly closed about these matters. I wanted to find out all about the Jewish holidays, but he said nothing. I would wonder, for example, why sometimes he would get a candle and light it and stick it in a jam jar. I would ask and he would simply say, 'Oh, it's a Jewish custom' – but he would never tell me about it. I used to say, 'Why do you do this if you don't believe in it?' And he would reply, 'In case my mother asks me.' It was only after some time that I came to learn that this was the *yohrtzeit* (memorial) candle for his late father.

In 1956 Maritta inherited her father's house in Vereker Road, West Kensington, although there were a number of complex legal problems to be overcome before she could take possession. Since it was already converted into flats, Maritta and Jack restricted themselves to redecorating it. But they soon became a formidable team in commerce as well as romance. For when Maritta inherited some money she immediately purchased a part-possession house at the Lots Road end of Chelsea, and with Jack set about converting it into flats.

One not unwelcome bonus to this romantic encounter was that enormous sums of money were made quite legitimately. But Jack was never in any doubt as to who was the driving force behind their commercial success. And although, according to Maritta, Jack had no imagination when it came to the décor, he could fairly claim:

I learned how to do some of the physical work, like plastering, rendering and so on. But Maritta was a very brilliant business-woman who could spot a house, do it up and sell it off at a vast profit. And not only was she brilliant commercially, she was also a highly talented artist and sculptress. My mother used to say about me, 'He's the one that's good with his hands', which was true, I suppose, but that's about all I was good for in relation to doing up those flats.

Bertha Preger certainly admired her son's new-found skill with his hands, but she was considerably less impressed with the manner in which he was handling his emotions. Not that Jack had discussed his relationship with her, for it was strictly taboo. Bertha's overriding fear was not at all difficult to detect: that her son and Maritta would marry. It was a fear that had a good deal of justification, even though all the evidence was strictly hearsay, and from a variety of sources. Her reaction to the prospect of a non-Jewish daughter-in-law was inspired by the time-honoured tradition among orthodox Jews whereby marrying a *shiksa*, a gentile woman, automatically entailed a period of ritualistic mourning for the 'bereaved' family. 'Marrying out' was viewed with such horror that the offending party was deemed to no longer exist.

It was a harsh penalty indeed. And as if the threat of being presumed dead was not bad enough, Bertha presented her son with a rather unpleasant ultimatum. However, since she was not prepared to confer 'recognition' on Jack's intended, it was an ultimatum that an intermediary was obliged to deliver. It fell to Leslie Preger, now a newly qualified general practitioner of medicine, to deliver Bertha's hidden trump card: that if Jack was to proceed and marry 'that girl' – the closest his mother could come to acknowledging Maritta's existence – then she would not hesitate to end her own life. Nor was Leslie an impartial go-between, for he too was deeply distressed by the prospect of Jack marrying out of the faith. What Bertha did not know, however, was that Jack's intended wife was every bit as tough as herself. It soon became clear: anything that the old lady could do, Maritta could do too, as Jack recollects:

On the one hand there was my mother saying that she would top herself if I got married – I mean, this was the good old days – and then Maritta made it quite clear that she would gas herself if I did not. Gassing yourself was fairly easy to carry out in those days, so it was a threat which I took entirely seriously.

With suicide threatened on both sides, Jack felt obliged to make a swift decision. Yet his reasoning hardly appeared to be satisfactory or sensible for one contemplating matrimony:

51

So I chose what I thought was the lesser of two evils and decided to marry Maritta. And as for 'marrying out' – it really wasn't an issue for me. My background of orthodox Judaism had long since gone. And likewise my commitment to the Zionist cause.

While Leslie kept his mother well briefed on his younger brother's intentions, Bertha decided to make one last-ditch appeal to her wayward son. Clearly, another tactic was required. This time it was in the form of a letter. Once again Bertha Preger did not mince her words:

3.10.55

Dear Jackie,

Before you tell me your decision I feel I want to write to you. I don't know if you have already made up your mind, or if what I have to say to you will make any impression on you. I only know that your question of who will suffer most cannot be answered by me. How can one measure or weigh pain and suffering? How can I foretell what losing you will do to me? How can I tell now – shocked and stupified as I am – what living here utterly alone, perhaps for years to come, will do to me? Daddy's death did not affect me till months later, when my mind went queer – and only by the grace of God and the necessity of letting you and Les finish your studies and provide a home for you all did I get better. But I feel I have not the same stamina or incentive to fight any more and therefore I just don't know. Your girl is young and youth has the power of recovery. I am no longer young.

Oh, I know I won't cast you off – you still remain my son – but my dear, inevitably you will cast yourself off. For how can it be otherwise? You will be free to come home whenever you wish, but how will you and your girl feel when you have to come alone. Your life will be withdrawn and I shall never know your wife or any children you may have. How can one measure all that when one loves one's son? I don't know. That's how I feel now. What the years will bring I can't foretell.

I beg you humbly to think hard to your own future happiness as well as ours.

Love
Mum

Jack tore the letter in half. And then in half again before throwing it in the wastepaper basket. Whereas previously he had been guilty of indecision, now his mind was made up. Of course Bertha was entitled to state her case. But Jack absolutely refused to submit this or any other prospective partner to a selection committee chaired by his mother and whose sole rationale was an overriding prejudice against all applicants not of the Jewish faith. No, Maritta would be his wife.

The wedding was not a grand affair. In fact it was not even a family affair. For not a single member of either family turned up at the Chelsea Registry Office on 23 November 1957 for the brief civil marriage. No one expected Bertha to attend the ceremony, but the absence of other family members was not entirely their own fault. Even if they had wanted to attend they would have had little chance to prepare for the celebrations, for it was only the week before that Maritta and Jack had finally decided to be wed. The only guests at the ceremony were Maritta's former nanny and a Miss Keyworth, one of Maritta's tenants. Even then, their presence was entirely practical: to act as witnesses. Maritta's mother was absent, as were Jack's brother and sister; and likewise a host of other relatives and friends from Manchester, Oxford and elsewhere. They were not present for one very compelling reason: they had not been asked to attend.

Despite contributing to Maritta's outstanding commercial success, Jack was far from being a wealthy man. Twenty-seven years of age on the day of his wedding, and his entire assets amounted to the meagre sum of ten shillings. So short of cash was he that the bride-to-be was obliged to advance Jack the money for a gold wedding ring.

The newly-weds honeymooned in Sussex for three days. Then, having piled all of their possessions onto a large trailer, they set off in a Landrover, heading west towards Wales. This was no idle excursion around the Welsh beauty spots. Jack and Maritta were embarking on a radically new lifestyle. The contrast with the world of property speculation could hardly have been more pronounced, as Maritta points out:

There was a feeling that we wanted to get away from the rat race. Jack had always loved farming, and I had spent a lot of my childhood in Wales and wanted to paint. A few months prior to our wedding I had looked at the map and showed Jack exactly where it was I thought we should live. I saw this remote spot and said to Jack, 'That is where I want to be.' There were no towns around and I could see from the map that there would be absolutely marvellous views down the coast. I just knew that I wanted to be out there on the headland, even though I had never been there before. We had been to Wales several times and even put in offers on some properties. When we looked at Gernos Farm for the first time Jack said, 'My goodness me, just look at that', because there was a mile of coastline and it really was in the most beautiful part of Wales. The farm was all shrouded in mist and rain – we didn't even know what was down there – we just looked into this swirling mist. Then a few days later I saw an ad in a farming paper for this very same farm, and we immediately decided to go ahead and buy it.

Maritta and Jack would surely have had difficulty in finding a more remote spot. Gernos Farm was situated at St Dogmaels in Pembrokeshire, and the nearest town was Cardigan in the adjoining county of Cardiganshire. The farm was about eighty acres, but together with some rough grazing along the cliffs it amounted to almost twice that amount. Much of it was difficult to farm, being steep and rocky. It was quite impossible to drive right up to the farm for the simple reason that there was no road, Gernos being situated a mile from the nearest approach road. And that was just the beginning of the farm. It came as no surprise to either Maritta or Jack to discover that Gernos had originally been part of the estate of a monastic order. The farmhouse itself was some considerable distance away and not far from a mile of cliffs and a six-hundred-foot drop down to the sea. The building itself, with massively thick walls, dated from the fourteenth century and had a chimney-piece made of ship's timbers.

The contrast between chic, sophisticated Chelsea and remote, rural Gernos could not have been more stark. There was no question about the breathtaking and spectacular nature of the landscape, but parts of the farm were so isolated that each year, from September until Easter, hardly a single soul would be seen. And for this vast domain the Pregers had needed to muster only £4000, scarcely more than the price of a London 'semi' in the mid-fifties. Maritta had provided the capital, although a substantial part of her estate remained tied up in converted flats for which purchasers had still to be found.

It was snowing when Maritta and Jack arrived to take possession of their new home. Not surprisingly, there was no welcoming delegation, only a number of cats who clearly thought that they had already laid claim to this inhospitable terrain. Yet the Pregers had two powerful resources with which to tackle this formidable new challenge: enthusiasm and love. Jack had always wanted to return to the land. Indeed, in his mind he had hardly left it. And it was Maritta who had chosen the spot with an instinct that had astounded her partner. Together they were bound to succeed.

Fit and strong, Jack had never been shy of manual labour. This was just as well because he would be obliged to load cow dung by hand and to spread it manually, for in the early days there was not enough capital to buy the machinery that would have alleviated the overwhelming tasks facing them. However, it was not long before contacts were made, and neighbouring farmers occasionally lent Jack more sophisticated machinery. Before long, too, he managed to purchase his own sheep and was rearing and selling cattle. It was back-breaking work. But it appeared to be succeeding.

As Jack continued to develop the farm, he found that he was able to grow crops where they had not been grown previously and to harvest them successfully. Although initially nervous about the scale of the undertaking, Jack became increasingly convinced that these early achievements would continue. The only real area of doubt was whether he would be able to sustain growth single-handed. Now, many years later, he looks back on the exhausting work at Gernos:

> I would do the milking twice a day for eighteen months on end. So if I got into town once a fortnight to do some shopping or buy spare parts I always had to rush back to do the milking in the evening. We did eventually have machines, but it wasn't just the milking. You had to bring the cows in, feed them, then get them out again, you had to feed the young stock, bring in some of the calves, lock some up for the night, feed the hens and so on. And there was always the milk to get out on top of all that, because we were very dependent on the monthly milk cheque. Sometimes in the snow you would have to go out through your neighbours' fields and the milk might be frozen solid and you would have to take and collect the milk every three days – just blocks of frozen milk. And in between all of this there would be all the work on the fields. I used to work very late in the winter time because I used to have to do the grinding of the corn after I'd finished the milking, and that would finish at about nine o'clock.

Small wonder that Jack became a sound sleeper. It might have been a constant fight against fatigue, but the atmosphere in the farmhouse was not at all unhappy. In their early days at Gernos there was no television, so what remained of the evenings would be spent discussing what had happened during the day, listening to Bach or Beethoven, preparing papers for submission to the Ministry of Agriculture and, if sufficient time and concentration remained, reading. There was a particularly good music shop in Cardigan of which Jack was a regular and highly valued customer, constantly indulging his passion for Segovia.

Maritta and Jack certainly shared a love of classical music, but there was no such readiness to share when it came to the work to be done on the farm. Indeed, the issue of who should do what began to place a severe strain on their marriage. The problem was that the allocation of tasks had never been properly clarified. Although it had been discussed on a number of occasions, Maritta and Jack still had radically different ideas of what had been agreed. Certainly Maritta was in no doubt:

> I got a guarantee from Jack that I wouldn't be expected to do any of the farm work. I have always been scared of cows – and evidently with some justification because Jack was once hurt by a cow kicking him across the shed. I never liked the farm work, although I did help him from time to time, for example sowing the corn, or with the livestock.

For Jack, such tinkering was simply not good enough. And as for the guarantee he was supposed to have furnished:

> There was no mention before we bought the farm that Maritta would not be helping at all. Normally on a farm like Gernos the wife helps with the milking, operates the milking machine or does the dairy cleaning. There came to be a lot of conflict over this farm work – I felt I'd been conned in that sense. She did back down a bit though; she went into a kind of market garden thing and she did pretty well at one stage – we were selling strawberries in Covent Garden. We used to send them by rail from Cardigan, but that was just about it so far as her effort towards the farm was concerned.

There was surely one obvious solution to this dispute, which had soon become a running sore within the marriage: to hire additional labour. Another pair of hands would have eased Jack's load considerably and enabled Maritta to pursue her other, more artistic, interests. She had always been attracted to the idea of the countryside rather than to the reality of toiling the land. And as Gernos Farm gradually became more established there would have been no problem paying another labourer. But Maritta was resolutely opposed to the idea, as Jack soon discovered:

> Gernos was quite simply a place which was impossible for one man to manage. But Maritta took a very strong stand on this issue. She didn't want a man working in the house and she didn't

want a girl particularly either. But I just had to have that help. Fortunately some other farmers in the area would send their man in from time to time to help me with the hay or with the harvest – and this would really save the day. On other occasions I would manage to persuade the postman when he'd finished his round to go on the back of the seed drill. But it was a hand-to-mouth existence and it just wouldn't do.

Maritta would in later years deny that she refused Jack a live-in labourer and insist that the only problem was finding a suitable candidate. It certainly was true that in such a remote location labourers were extremely difficult to come by. Even so, it was now apparent that their marriage was disintegrating very rapidly indeed.

As if these pressures were not enough, there remained the issue of Bertha. Jack had taken a stand, true, and ignored his mother's dire threats and warnings, the most serious of which had not come to fruition. But the old lady was still very much alive and kicking, as Maritta was about to discover. For almost a year and a half from the date of their marriage Bertha maintained limited contact, telephoning Jack every Friday night. The ritual was invariably the same. Maritta would answer the telephone. There would follow a courteous, if somewhat brief, request to speak to Jack. Such remained the relationship between Bertha and her daughter-in-law until Bertha's visit to Gernos in July 1959, which Maritta has reason to recall vividly:

When Jack's mother arrived she had these beady brown eyes and gave me a cold look, full of hatred. I have never received a stonier look, one more full of hatred than that first glance which Bertha cast over me. She was freezing with me and spent all her time talking about Leslie. It was the sort of conversation which you would have had with someone if you got chatting in a dentist's waiting room, terribly artificial and contrived. It was Jack's birthday and I had made and decorated a cake which I remember she went out of her way to criticize, announcing that it had looked quite plain. All family subjects were therefore not talked about. It was just 'Leslie this and Leslie that' all the time – the good son, the doctor who had not 'married out' and let his mother down so.

Would Bertha have behaved quite so frostily had she known that Maritta was carrying her first grandchild? In fact, at the time, none of those seated around that rather sad farmhouse table knew of Maritta's condition. For she was a little under one month pregnant but still to discover the fact. When, a few weeks later, she informed Jack, both were delighted at the prospect of becoming parents for the first time.

On 14 April 1960 Maritta gave birth to a son. But far from bringing Maritta and Jack closer together, the arrival into the world of little Alun Preger seemed to have the opposite effect. Maritta puts it rather succinctly:

Our marriage went down the drain as soon as Alun was born. I had no hot water for the first six months of Alun's life. In fact sometimes we had no water at all because our twenty or so cows would drink it after their feed and divert it from us. Jack needed hot water for the dairy. I needed it for Alun's nappies, and there were continual rows about this. You could almost say that our marriage broke up over hot water. Of course, it would have been a lot quicker to have got a plumber. But no plumber ever arrived.

When Jack saw Alun for the first time his reaction was somewhat bizarre. His words were hardly an outpouring of paternal love: 'Poor little thing, when you think of all he's got to go through.' This was certainly not a reference to the prospect of a ritualistic circumcision during the following eight days, as required by Jewish law, for Jack was vehemently opposed to the practice. This rather baffled his wife, who would later confess to forming the impression that Jack was somewhat anti-Semitic.

Maritta's grievances grew ever stronger:

Once Alun was born I think that Jack felt that he came second. But Jack always had to come first. He would hardly ever touch Alun and certainly he never changed a nappy. Since he was always more interested in running the farm than in the new-born child, there was never any relationship as such between them. In addition to all of this the cottage was extremely small, with just two tiny bedrooms upstairs. The one Alun had was damp – his top blanket would have moisture on it when I would go in in the mornings. The cottage was continually damp but for the first couple of years I didn't mind, because the idea was that we would build a proper marital home on the farm with the proceeds of our London properties. In the end I said, you must make up your mind. We needed a proper house for a child to grow up in. I wanted to built a house at Gernos, up on the top. I would have done all of the decorating myself.

In the event no decorating was done because no house was built. Just as Maritta had been opposed to the hiring of additional labour, so Jack took a firm stand against the construction of Maritta's dream home:

The house was a real bone of contention. I didn't object to the house as such – it was just that it was in a very difficult position. It was quite impossible to get up there by normal traffic – a Landrover couldn't get up except if you reversed it. Then there were these hairpin bends – you had to drive into these hairpin bends, reverse up the next stretch and into the next hairpin, then drive forward again; that's what the approach was like. We did start taking the stones up there, because Maritta was adamant that the house be built of stones, and they were in piles up at the top of the farm at the edge of a big field, there for the whole of the neighbourhood to see, this heap of stones – Maritta's mad folly.

And what of Bertha, the new grandmother? If there was any change at all in her stubborn posture, it was really only in the slightest degree, as Maritta explains:

After Bertha's visit to Gernos she wrote to Jack and asked him to thank me for my hospitality, but that was all. Things only changed once I had delivered a live and healthy grandson. She then announced to Jack that whereas previously she had asked to speak to Jack immediately, she was now prepared to speak to me on a Friday night. Big deal! But I did realize that it was difficult for her. I was aware of her upbringing and her flight from Germany. I just had to consider that it was her loss, which it was. In any event there was little I could do.

It was true: there was little that could be done about Bertha and her prejudices. But as far as her relationship with Jack was concerned Maritta was not cast in that same, passive role. By the time Alun was two and a half Maritta had had enough. Nothing had changed. There was little prospect of the new home ever being built. The issue of additional labour was unresolved. Even the plumbing had not been attended to satisfactorily. Little remained of the love and enthusiasm with which they had arrived at Gernos five years earlier. Now Maritta was in no doubt: she would be better off in London, managing her portfolio of properties. She would not return to Gernos unless there existed a serious undertaking to build that home. Until that time she would absent herself. And as for Alun the question of leaving him with his father simply did not arise. But even though, as Maritta admits, she had no real intention at the time of leaving Gernos for good, this de facto separation was the beginning of the end for the Pregers' fragile marriage. It also spelled the end of a father's relationship with his son, as Jack recalls:

When Maritta went off to London there were these prolonged separations, and they would really gnaw away at me. I had a very bad time over Alun, and couldn't bear the separations. I used to go and see them once in a while – they were living at a place called Railway Cottages at Barnes. One difficulty was having to arrange a relief milker, but I found when I came back from being with them I was in real trouble. Not from missing Maritta – I could manage without her – but I used to miss Alun so much. He was about three or four years old by then and extremely cute and I loved him very much. I used to miss him so much that I couldn't eat for a week each time I returned, and I used to live on black tea and dry toast because I found that I just wasn't able to digest anything – and this became a regular occurrence. I couldn't eat. I couldn't sleep. I used to have to force myself to work on the farm. In the end I decided that I had to stop going to London because I just couldn't take this week of suffering afterwards.

Jack was not the only one to suffer. Alun was hurting too, and for a good deal more than just one week at a time. On the few occasions when Alun did see his father he used all the means at a small child's disposal to convey to him an urgent message of unconditional love. For Maritta, who would observe these small dramas unfold, it was a truly pitiful sight:

> Jack's attitude was that it was much the best if he should have no contact with Alun – 'for him to forget me', as he used to put it. But of course children do not forget their parents. Alun would often ask, 'Well, where's MY daddy, MY daddy?' I remember once when he was a child we had a worker in the house and Alun announced, 'That's daddy', which was most embarrassing for me. Alun was always wildly excited every time he used to see Jack. He would always sit on his lap and with real feeling announce, 'Daddy – I love you – I love you', almost as if he was trying to get through to him and shake this revelation into Jack's mind. But Jack would just sit there with his pipe and say, 'All right, all right, I know.' This used to be so very upsetting for me – Alun would throw his arms around his daddy – and there was never any response from Jack even though Alun was so desperate for it, and this would just bring a lump to my throat.

Having had the opportunity to reconsider her position while in London, Maritta came to the conclusion that perhaps the marriage could be salvaged after all. Not so Jack. For when Maritta finally did offer to return, Jack refused outright. His reason was by no means original: it was too late – someone else had come along.

Catherine Wells was of Catholic stock, the daughter of William Wells, then a Member of Parliament for a Midlands constituency, a Queen's Counsel and senior member of the Bar. When Jack met Cathy for the first time in the summer of 1964 she was nineteen and he fifteen years older. Once again Jack had fallen for an art student. Cathy had seen an advertisement placed by Jack in her art school's students' union. It was an opportunity to do some agricultural work during the summer – Jack's solution to the vexed issue of additional labour. Nowadays Cathy insists:

> I don't want to go into the dramatic love side of it, because it all sounds rather improbable now when you look back on it. Suffice it to say that we were very fond of each other for a long time. But in the end he was to upset the course of my life. My first impression of Jack, though, was that he was a nice, funny man, although I did notice that he could suddenly become very aggressive. I did not meet Maritta at Gernos, because she had already been gone for about a year by the time I arrived. I stayed one week on that first visit.

Jack was not at all certain that he wanted the relationship with Cathy to continue. For many years he would dither and delay. But when Cathy returned to London to pursue her studies, Jack became convinced that his marriage to Maritta had to come to an end. As he put it in a brutally frank letter from Gernos:

> 17 August 1964
>
> Dear Maritta,
> I'm afraid that I feel it essential to end our marriage now. Perhaps you would let me know in due course how you would wish our business affairs to be wound up. My solicitors will be Williams and Davies (Mr Walters).
>   Please give my love to Alun.
>
> Yours,
> Jack.

Maritta confesses:

> This note came as a bolt from the blue. But I didn't take too much notice of it, because I knew full well what Jack was like.

Goodness me, I'd received another letter only weeks earlier in which he announced that he had signed a contract with a builder for the construction of the house, with completion guaranteed for the August of 1965. Then there was another note in which Jack said that he 'felt awful' about Alun and still another in which he said that 'I might still find myself eating humble pie.' One minute he would be phoning the architect to announce that the house was definitely on. And the next minute that it was off. This chopping and changing was typical of Jack – I don't know if it's depression or schizophrenia or what it is.

Gernos might well have been associated in Maritta's mind with depression and divorce. But it was the setting for a series of triumphs too. These were mostly the result of extremely hard physical work, as Jack recounts:

When things went right for you, it would be fantastic – for example when the harvest was good. For years I had machines which could only be classified as absolute rubbish. They were second-hand and I used to spend hours stripping them down and trying to get them to work properly. Gradually though I got better machines, often from the Cooperative Society in Cardigan where I used to buy my fertilizer and just about everything else. When the machines were properly adjusted I would really tear through the farm work. And then I went down to this big estate sale in Pembrokeshire where there was a combine harvester which no one wanted. It was a very good make and I lashed out £175. It was a beauty and nobody could believe that I could harvest these crops on this impossible farm with that combine harvester. So I did have these good times too.

Visitors to Gernos were few and far between. Not that Gernos never heard laughter. A considerable part of these lighter moments was associated with a Catholic priest called Shaemus Cunnane and a drunken Welsh tramp, John Clarke, known by most as Dai. On Cathy's visits to Gernos, Jack would drive her to Mass in the Catholic church in Cardigan. Still firmly agnostic, Jack would wait patiently outside in his Landrover. It was on one such visit to Cardigan that Father Cunnane approached him. Not only was it the beginning of an enduring friendship, it was an encounter that would in time fundamentally transform Jack's life. Father Cunnane:

> I came to Cardigan in the January of 1962, by which time Jack was already farming at Gernos. It was nice to meet someone with brains – Jack is most certainly an intellectual. I only got to know him properly though when once the police rang me saying that they had a chap who was threatening to commit more crime and who would be going back to jail if he couldn't be sorted out. They asked if I might be able to help. John Clarke had led a very strange life, in and out of jail. I thought to myself, Who is the best Christian in this area? – and I immediately thought of this non-practising Jew at Gernos. I just felt sure that he would be far more willing to help than all my Christian parishioners. And I was right.

Jack was delighted to be able to help. True, it was doing the priest a good turn. But here was an unexpected source of labour, someone who might be able to accept the isolation of Gernos and its tough working conditions. Dai was a down-and-out with a history of alcohol abuse and a very nasty temper that was on occasion quite violent. Although Dai was a little simple, it was an arrangement that was to work well for a considerable time. In fact Dai was more than a little simple, as Jack soon discovered:

> Having Dai around did enable me to concentrate on working out in the fields. I decided to leave him to man the kitchens, which he seemed able to manage. I used to get various tinned puddings from the grocer, most of which were on special offer, probably because they had seen their finest hour. Perhaps I should have been more specific with my instructions because I remember coming in for lunch once only to find Dai in a state of shock. Of course he should have pierced the lids of these tins and put them in a pan of water, but he had just put them on top of the very hot stove. After about fifteen minutes one had exploded, evicting half

of its contents onto the ceiling. But Dai clearly didn't believe in wasting anything, so he set about scraping it off. He did get to the other tins before they too went off, but I found that I just couldn't bring myself to explain what he had done wrong. I simply said, 'Dear, dear, we really were a bit lucky there Dai, only one of the three tins going off like that.'

But Jack was not having much fun. True, there were bouts of frivolity and the odd opportunity for a classic Preger prank. It was all rather reminiscent of the personality pattern that had first revealed itself at Oxford: up one moment and down the next. In fact at Gernos there was enough to make anyone depressed, let alone someone with a tendency to mental instability. And the fuel firing that gloom was a desperate, overriding sense of loneliness and isolation that, joker though he was, Jack could not hide. He explains:

> There was one occasion when I had been snowed up absolutely alone for three months. I did not see a soul. Maritta had gone. Alun had gone. Even my supply of casual labourers had dried up, Dai having moved on. There seemed to be this pointlessness in farming, because no matter how hard you worked, in the end the prices of the produce still seemed to fall every year, and I began to think it was impossible to see any future commercially at Gernos. After being snowed up I'd no reserves at all of any crop whatsoever and some of the stock were so weak they could hardly stand up. I was feeding them on the bottom of haystacks.

Jack needed help. He was seeking an intervention of a radical nature:

> It was this loneliness and lack of future that made me pray for something to believe in. I then did one of those very dangerous things. I prayed to God to give me just one sign of His existence, to show me just one single thing. To be honest, I didn't even know to whom or to what or for what I was praying. Yet I made a kind of bargain: that if I was given one thing that I could say is a

sign of God's existence, then I would spend the rest of my life in His service.

The outcome of this accord was that Jack Preger would indeed spend the remainder of his life serving not the land but the Lord. Gernos Farm might not always have provided sufficient fodder. But in the end it would yield an abundant supply of faith.

5

'It's the legacy of the Jewish prophets'

It was clear that Jack needed to believe. But in what? There were few clues as to the direction in which he might be heading. One thing alone was certain: Jack's constant quest for spirituality had succeeded only in further confusing his estranged wife, as she confirms:

> On the farm Jack was completely atheistic. Actually, he was always deriding Catholicism in particular, and he used to delight in mimicking old Keyworth, my former nanny, who was a devout Catholic. He was always asking how all the stars had come to be there, constantly asking these penetrating philosophical questions. It was hardly as if I had the answers – I had not even resolved the issue of my supply of hot water! He used to read the *New Scientist* – in fact Jack was constantly reading. After some time, though, I used to feel that he was a bit like a black hole, absorbing all this information, but without anything ever seeming to come out.

But she was wrong. Although Maritta was not there to witness her husband's outpouring of faith, perhaps she should not have been quite so surprised when it eventually occurred. For she had been at Gernos when Jack had returned from town one day, proudly clutching a Bible he had purchased from a second-hand bookshop in Cardigan. That Bible had rapidly become a permanent fixture on the large kitchen table at which all meals were eaten in the farm-house. And it would in due course propel Jack Preger away from the peace and tranquillity of the Pembrokeshire coast, to the chaos and confusion of the backstreets of Calcutta. Jack explains how his conversion came about:

> It was true that I was lonely on the farm. But I was not ready to drift into anything – to become an orthodox Jew, for example. It was the New Testament that I was discovering. I was reading it every day and it was a revelation to me, a teaching of philosophy, if you like. As I would read through the Bible, time and again I came to realize that these teachings obviously didn't come from any ordinary person, certainly not an ordinary carpenter's son in Palestine. Of course the Old Testament was there too – but it was Christ I was discovering.

Jacob Preger, formerly of the Manchester Yeshiva, was discovering Christ. Since this was such a dramatic departure from his strictly orthodox Jewish roots, it was perhaps not unreasonable for Preger to seek firm proof that the Almighty did indeed exist. Once again it was the Bible that was able to satisfy his needs:

> I had been reading the Bible. But this time I made a demand. I said, 'You open the page for me. I'm not going to open it – You show me.' That was the sign I wanted. 'Show me something in here that shows me that You exist.' And then an extraordinary thing happened: I turned to a part of the Bible that I did not remember ever having read before. Certainly I had no familiarity with that section when I came to it. It was St Paul. Now, when I came to that particular part I actually felt a force drawing my finger down the page.

Preger had stumbled on two short paragraphs from Romans 11:25–6, a letter from St Paul to the Romans. The sixty-five words contained in those paragraphs, which were to have such a remark able impact on Jack, are:

25 For I would not, brethren, that ye should be ignorant of this mystery, lest ye should be wise in your own conceits; that blindness in part is happened to Israel, until the fulness of the Gentiles be come in.

26 And so all Israel shall be saved: as it is written, There shall come out of Sion the Deliverer, and shall turn away ungodliness from Jacob.

St Paul's letter stated categorically that darkness had fallen upon Israel. The message could hardly have been clearer: until the Jews become reconciled with the Church of Christ, they will not be saved. Since the text also referred specifically to the family of Jacob, the given name appearing on all of Preger's official documents, he considered that here was a message directed towards him personally and one that he ought now to heed. For Preger, it was simply too much to attribute it to coincidence: 'I felt deeply moved by this. The challenge I had laid down had been met to my entire satisfaction.'

Here was the sign for which Preger had been searching. Here, the answer to his prayers. It was a sign of sufficient power and energy for him to do as St Paul exhorted: to become a Christian and dispense with any remaining attachment to the Judaism of his youth. Just as Saul had converted from Judaism and become Paul, it was time now for Jacob to become Jack.

And who better to facilitate and oversee such a transformation than Jack's friend, Father Cunnane? To the Irish priest, the leap from Judaism to Catholicism was not as dramatic or radical as many might think. As Father Cunnane sees it:

What St Paul is basically saying is that the church is Jewish, always has been Jewish and cannot be anything else but Jewish, which is something which has long been forgotten. I do appreciate that this would be hateful to an orthodox Jew, but when St Paul speaks in the Bible words like: 'Neither, because they are the seed of Abraham, are they all children; but, In Isaac shall thy seed be called', he is saying that we Christians are in fact the continuation of the chosen people. Many Jews bring a kind of curtain down when you mention Christ. They won't recognize him or study him. But I soon discovered, when working with Jack, that he didn't limit himself in this way.

The incident with the Bible was not the first mystical experience to which Jack had been party, for a few months earlier, in March 1964, Gernos had provided the setting for a most remarkable encounter. Preger had been working out in the open, carting cow dung from the yard up to the fields with the assistance of a tractor and muckspreader. Seldom did the ritual change; up and down the field he would go, spread the dung and come back again for more. He would repeat this tedious pattern so many times that he soon acquired the knack of being able to work automatically. While his body diligently performed the tasks requiring to be done, his mind was free to drift off in any number of other directions.

> I found one day that my mind was floating away – not that there was any danger with the machine, mind you. I had found that the driving had become second nature. I was just coming round the beginning of the hairpin bends – I know the exact position on the road when it happened. It was barely evening and there was a gateway looking out over the sea. Suddenly, I felt that my head was being opened and the message 'Become a doctor' was put in. It was not a voice or a sound. Just the thought. And then I felt my head being closed up again.

Whatever the source of that message, it was an injunction that Jack acted on rapidly. For that evening, having finished the day's tasks, he sat down at the farmhouse table and wrote letters of application to half a dozen medical schools and teaching hospitals, assuring them of his earnest desire to qualify as a doctor. Now, the thirty-four-year-old graduate farmer's mind was made up: it would take several years, of course, but one day, in the not too distant future, it would be Jack Preger, MD.

In fact it would be Jack Declan Preger, MD – the name that would later appear on his official baptismal certificate, awarded on completion of his instruction. This self-given middle name, with its deeply Catholic and Irish overtones, is so far removed from Jack's original Hebrew name – Yaacob Ben Zviaryia – that it is perhaps as well to ask once again: were there any other significant events or experiences responsible for bringing about such a radical departure from his firm roots in Mancunian Jewry? Jack's adoption of a new middle name has its own explanation, as we shall see later. But as for the present formula for conversion, the chief component was the loving kindness demonstrated by Father Cunnane. Jack has never forgotten what it was that brought him to embrace Christ. In a letter to the priest, he was proud to admit that: ' . . . the thing that initially attracted me to the Church in Cardigan was the sense of charity and community in you . . . especially in sending Dai and other strays to Gernos . . . '.

True, Preger was also influenced by writers such as Evelyn Waugh and Graham Greene, in whose novels there figures a strong thread of Catholicism. But could a combination of literature and Christian charity be enough to explain both Jack's conversion and his later commitment to the poor? To Father Cunnane, the answer is quite clear. It might be part of the truth. But only part. In reviewing Frances Meigh's book *The Jack Preger Story*, Cunnane sets out his case:

What has gone to make him the man he is? Where does his social conscience come from? What has given him his amazing stubborness in the face of persecution that would long since have driven others away from Calcutta? We hear little of that from the author. To me the answers are plain, for I saw those traits in him before he sought baptism. They are from his Jewish background, a culture that has made a contribution to the world out of all proportion to its size. Dr Jack Preger has a social conscience? Read the prophet Amos and see where it came from. The West Bengalis think he is arrogant? Jews are used to wrestling with God; if you can do that, Indian officials are nothing . . .

'It's the legacy of the Jewish prophets'

As the priest explains:

> What I was trying to say in that review was that that experience on the tractor had to operate on something. And in my opinion what it operated on was a good, old-fashioned, straight-down-the-line Jewish attitude towards the dignity of human beings, human rights and so on. You know, some of the old radicals and socialists from the Jewish community, people like Manny Shinwell. So I'm in no doubt – it's the legacy of the Jewish prophets, especially Amos, in my opinion, who told the people of Samaria, as did Isaiah, about the way they were treating the poor. Whatever this religious experience Jack had – and I do believe that he had it – that's the base material it was working on . . .

Cunnane might have been sure about the precise nature of Preger's 'base material'. Yet Jack soon became preoccupied with dispensing with it in its entirety and in proceeding with his conversion to Catholicism as rapidly as possible. When he approached Father Cunnane to see if he might be able to take instruction, the priest was more than happy to oblige:

> I must be honest and say that I'm still not quite sure what made Jack turn towards the Catholic church – because I don't consider myself to be a great advertisement for it. But I have to tell you that I found working with Jack extremely exhilarating. I gave him several talks about the nature of Catholicism. Jack is one of those people with whom you just have to start a sentence and he can finish it for you – he's that intelligent. And secondly we are a Semitic religion, and normally it's hard to get people to see Christianity prefigured in Judaism. Of course Jack cottoned onto everything straight away. In fact I have to say that talking to Jack about the complex relationship between Judaism and Christianity was one of the most exciting experiences of my entire life.

In the event Jack would complete the process of instruction in Ireland rather than Wales. And it was from Dublin, in 1965, that he would write to Father Cunnane about the formidable problems of erasing earlier religious imprints:

> I approached a chaplain for religious instruction and had one session with him before he went off to the Council of Europe at Vienna. So I go now to St Kevin's, but it's very intensive. About an hour a week is what I had in mind. But the first session went on for two hours and I keep being told to come back again! This week I have three sessions. Actually, I'm very glad it's working out like this since there is so much ground to cover. We've gone back (again!) to the start of the Catechism and it seems just as rewarding as when I was with you. I'm beginning to understand a little of what is implied by even trying to become a Catholic. It's quite strange emptying one's mind at my age and starting afresh.

Barely six weeks later he was again complaining to the priest about the arduous task before him. Converting to Catholicism was not quite as easy or straightforward as he had thought. Still, at least there were no distractions of an agricultural nature:

> And now . . . I have to face Fr Tonge for my weekly session; only sometimes it's bi-weekly and the 'hour' is the most elastic yet encountered. But my timekeeping has improved – no cows etc., and just step across the road. Civilization!

Was Jack really emptying his mind and starting afresh? Probably not. More likely he was reorganizing and reappraising material of which he already had a measure of understanding from many hours' study of the Talmud. It was true that Jack was converting to Christianity, a process utterly incomprehensible, if not grotesque, to most Jews. But that was not how Jack viewed it. On the contrary, he considered that he was really discovering a new approach to Judaism.

> What most Jews tend to forget is that so many of the people in the New Testament were Jews. Miriam, the mother of God – as the Jews refer to Mary – and Jesus to the extent that he lived as a

person, were both Jews. Christ was a Jew and he died as a Jew. The last supper was a Pesach, the Jewish Passover. Christ never sought to deny his Judaism and stated that he was an orthodox Jew. All too often it is forgotten that Christ was not a Christian but a Jew. This might sound like a cliché, but it is possible that when you discover Christ and his message, you may end up by being more Jewish than you were before.

Leslie Preger would have none of this. Only much later would he learn of his brother's conversion to Catholicism, by which time he had emigrated to America and was making rapid progress in the field of medicine. He was surprised to discover that Jack had become a Catholic, but not astonished:

I was aware that Jack had this tendency to have strong feelings in favour of something or other, so it was not difficult to see him changing streams. It seems to me, though, that Jack could just as easily have become a Marxist as a Catholic. I would just like to know what he found wanting in Judaism. Remember that Jack's intellectual knowledge of Judaism is based on the intellectual level of a fifteen-year-old boy – when he left the Manchester Yeshiva – whereas his intellectual knowledge of Catholicism is that of a mature man. So the odds are not quite even.

Jack was taking to Catholic theology like a duck to water. But from the perspective of the Catholic authorities he was by no means a prize catch. The reason for this was that he was in the throes of rather acrimonious divorce proceedings. And worse still, from the priests' point of view, he did not exclude the possibility of one day remarrying in church. In fact when Father Cunnane refused to issue a nullity decree in respect of his marriage to Maritta, Jack did not like it one bit, as the priest recalls:

The thing is, we don't just hand out nullity decrees like sweets. This didn't go down well with Jack, who walked out on me, slamming the door as he left. Of course I was upset at this, because I thought that I had lost a good friend. I didn't see Jack

75

for some three months after that incident. Then, one day, he came back and said that when he had cooled down after our row he had decided that I was right, and what he had regarded as moral principles were in fact just emotions.

And why was Jack so eager to be rid of Maritta? Was it to enable him to marry Cathy? Certainly their relationship was thriving, and yet, as Maritta explains:

> I had an inkling that Jack was up to something. I was still living with Alun in our small cottage in Barnes. Jack didn't mention anything about becoming a Catholic or this business about wanting to qualify as a doctor. I wouldn't have minded all that. What I did object to was another woman, and on one of his visits to London I went through his pockets, like all good wives, and sure enough there was a letter from Cathy. I challenged Jack about this letter and he immediately admitted that there was another woman.

Shortly before the divorce proceedings were finalized, Maritta received the most unexpected of all callers – Cathy. She had come with a specific purpose: to plead with Maritta to grant Jack a divorce. Maritta was delighted to be able to put Cathy more fully in the picture, expressing surprise that she did not know the divorce was almost through. As Maritta recalls:

> In other words, Jack had been saying that I was the one who had been refusing him a divorce and it was therefore me who was preventing their romance from blossoming into matrimony.

Cathy went on with what she had come to say:

'I've read all of your diaries and come to the conclusion that you could not be as bad as Jack said you were.'

Maritta was so taken aback by this remark that she was not at all sure how to reply. The best she was able to manage in the circumstances was a rather feeble, 'Oh, thank you very much.'

As if turning up unexpectedly at Maritta's home was not outrageous enough, the student of art, still only twenty-one, sent the following letter a few weeks later. It is laced with dramatic irony, as will later become apparent:

17 November 1966
Dear Maritta,
I was not intending to start a long acquaintance when I arrived rather rudely on your doorstep. But I've been grateful that you were civil as well as outspoken. I am still not trying to prolong correspondence, but I've something more to say.

I'm not taking an exalted position. I'm not one to see a 'case' clearly except momentarily, fluctuating, or in an argument. Jack *is* a man who has wronged Alun and you and me and others too perhaps. He is an idealist, too.

His mind, dazzled by the 'great good' he can do as a doctor, negates other people's private feelings, and distorts his own feelings because he would rather have them out of the way and therefore does not examine them with scrupulous honesty, as everyone should. Unfortunately for him, he is still human. This, you see too.

I'm going off at a tangent now. What brought me onto this was Alun. Jack does care for him and obviously trusts you to bring him up. He was upset when he realized that Alun was aware of his inadequacy, because people generally do desire the approval of children. Jack, no exception, was gratified when Alun used to think he was marvellous. Both are worse off now that Alun feels there's something wrong with his father. Jack becomes more irritated by the situation because guilt, which interferes with his idea of doing good, presents itself in Alun, for although he trusts you with Alun's security, affection and childish education, yet he does not trust you to support him (Jack) all the way along the line to be as useful to society as he sees it (numerically), as he possibly can.

So Jack plays down concern for Alun and loses patience with him. He thinks that tied to Alun and you he would be weakened, not by the responsibility, but in his purpose and its ultimate fruition. He feels too weak to hold out against human affections

77

which in him are so strongly emotional. Meanwhile, Alun, who like all children wants to admire grown-ups, will not see Jack as a fallible human until he is much, much older and by then, unless something is changed in the present range of information about his father, he might really be deprived. This is what my long bumbling epistle is about. If you, you especially, lamely agree that 'Daddy should be here' . . . If you do not give him the impression that Daddy cares . . . (If he overhears you utter the words: 'Daddy does not care' — 'He doesn't care for him', anything like that), he's a sensitive child, he'll blame himself. He is incapable of dividing himself from his father's image. At this point it would be useless to explain that Jack is no good as a father. You will simply have to say that Daddy has other things to do, lots of sick people to look after and that he trusts you to look after him and give him the time he isn't able to give him, but would like to.

I cannot say any more; I have already put my foot in too far where it is not my place; it is only my thought.

Yours sincerely,

Cathy

Cathy had indeed put her foot in it. Maritta, seething with resentment and disbelief at the prize cheek of her husband's young love who so unhesitatingly issued unsolicited advice about the upbringing of her son, was not at all sure how to respond. In fact she made no response at all, simply digesting her own disgust and fury.

The teachings of Christ might well have a good deal to say about the sanctity of family life and the obligations of parents to their offspring, but this was an area to which Jack paid scant regard. Not just theologically, but in practical terms too. For although he made a series of trips to London to see Alun, each visit was more distressing than the previous one. On one occasion a row developed over an issue that could hardly have been more trivial. Alun, always understandably excited to see his father, would embark on any number of strategies in order to be the permanent beneficiary of Jack's attention during these brief visits. On one such occasion he thought that this might best be achieved by turning off the lights while his father was taking a bath. Storming out of the bathroom to remedy the situation, Jack slammed the door, and in so doing hurt his son's hand quite badly. Although the child was inconsolable for a short time, Jack's response was to absent himself from the house. It was to be an absence of almost six years. The next time Alun would see his father would be when he was a little over eleven years of age.

The boy's uncle Leslie did what he could:

I didn't like to see the kid without a father, so when I came back to London I used to see Alun every now and then. I would take him out to Madame Tussaud's, to London Zoo and so on. But of course my occasional visits were no substitute for a father's presence.

For a number of years Jack embarked on what can only be described as a bizarre kind of double life, at least in terms of religious adherence. Converting to Catholicism was not an overnight process, and during the years of his instruction Jack would regularly visit his widowed mother. How did Bertha react to the prospect of her son becoming a Catholic? In fact she was to have no reaction at all, for the very simple reason that she would never learn about Jack's disenchantment with Judaism. For he decided it was best to say nothing at all, displaying a subtle blend of sensitivity to his mother's feelings and a natural desire to protect his own:

I just didn't think she could take it. I'd already married out of the faith once, and I came to the conclusion that these matters were best kept off the agenda during my visits home.

The extent to which Jack was prepared to act out this diplomatic charade was extraordinary. He found that the most satisfactory solution was to pretend that in terms of his religious beliefs nothing much had changed. It was in this spirit of economy with the truth that Jack found himself able, during a traditional Friday night meal, not just to don skullcap and prayer shawl but to recite the entire *baruchas* for the ushering in of the Sabbath, as required by Jewish law. Moreover, he could switch allegiance with startling rapidity, having no difficulty in reciting ancient Hebrew prayers one day and attending Mass the next.

Nor was Jack the only one to pretend that unpalatable truths did not exist. Others, too, were party to this conspiracy of silence, as Anita confesses:

> We all went along with this game, you see. As far as my father's family were concerned, the first child and the first marriage just did not exist. Mother never ever discussed it. Of course Maritta manifestly did exist, but not in our lives. Even now, all these years on, my daughter Heidi lives in London, which is where Alun also happens to live. They are first cousins, but they have absolutely no knowledge whatsoever of each other's existence, let alone any contact with one other.

Nonetheless, Jack was pursuing his conversion with his familiar blend of energy and vigour. In 1966 he was baptized, and the following year saw his confirmation. While he was otherwise able to take Catholic theology entirely seriously, he found great difficulty in doing so during these ceremonies. Confident and comfortable with his new faith, he felt that there was simply no need for it to be publicly confirmed. To Jack, many of the ceremonies were both hollow and absurd:

> Being baptized and then confirmed was a ghastly business. Because you had all these chaps who had been converted – presumably because they were Protestants. We were all about the same age and attending this ceremony performed by the Archbishop of Dublin, who was a great disciplinarian. All these other fellows were crossing themselves compulsively, when I'm quite sure there was no need to cross yourself. I suppose they had seen Catholics crossing themselves and thought that this was the thing to do. It was the same sense of embarrassment that I used to feel during Jewish rituals. And then I thought to myself, What on earth am I doing here, performing this rapid crossing movement? – it just doesn't mean anything to me.

'It's the legacy of the Jewish prophets'

From the outset, Preger's Catholicism was eclectic. And he had as much difficulty with the concept of communion as he did with the ritual itself. During communion Catholics are required to believe that when they swallow the wafer and it is blessed by the priest, they are receiving the body and blood and love of Jesus Christ. It might be a central part of Catholic orthodoxy, but it cut no ice with Preger and was therefore dispensed with. As was confession. One bad experience of it was enough to put him off for life:

> I went to confession on one occasion and the priest's reaction to what I had to say struck me as so appalling I knew immediately that I would never go to confession again as long as I lived – or until perhaps I was on my deathbed. Because it just seemed such nonsense what he had told me. I thought to myself, Well, if that's what the Catholic church is offering, then I'm just not interested in going through that whole rigmarole again.

So while Jack became a practising Catholic, he had strong and non-conformist views on communion and confession. What, then, of that other tenet of Catholicism, the concept of papal infallibility. Once again Jack was far from impressed:

> I don't believe in it at all. As far as I am concerned, the Pope is just an elected member of the Vatican establishment. He's not going to tell me, with absolute certainty, what we should all be believing. For example, if the Pope said that he had been fasting for forty days and forty nights and that he had seen this incredible vision – that it was the Virgin Mary, and that she had told him that she is seated at the right hand of God, I would say, 'Well, good for you, but that might just be a product of your fasting and prayer.' It might be true for him or it might just be nonsense. But there's certainly no question of infallibility about it.

If there is one notion capable of uniting the many hundreds of millions of Catholics around the world, it is their persistent and vociferous opposition to abortion. But exclude Preger from their number:

81

What might be true in the West – that the life of the foetus is so precious – isn't necessarily true out in the East. First of all I can't believe that a Church which has been able to kill so many people in the past for doctrinal reasons, can suddenly develop such an interest in the foetus, or that the foetus could become so holy. What is so holy about the foetus, when the Church has no difficulty in tolerating all sorts of atrocities in all kinds of prisons and police stations all over the world? What's the difference between the foetus in the womb and a prisoner in a cell as far as God is concerned?

Preger took instruction for a number of years in order to become a Catholic. Once a Catholic, he appeared to swiftly repudiate a substantial part of many of the notions central to it. What processes were going on in his mind to make this come about? Father Cunnane perhaps comes close to an explanation:

When St Francis of Assisi was alive he was just as much a Catholic as the Pope, but he lived rather differently. It was going to be a bit like that with Jack. I thought to myself, He's got to do this, he's being driven to do this, and there's no way that anyone will tell him what he should be doing. Jack is by nature one of the world's loners – he cannot fit into anyone else's organization, it's disastrous if he tries. I realized during the time he took instruction with me that nobody can control him, he's off on his own. He obviously believes, but there is no way that Jack is going to believe exactly along the straight lines that I do. Yes, Jack has received some kind of a message from God – I've no doubt about that – but I'm blowed if I know what it is.

Refusing to blindly accept every aspect of Catholicism, Preger embraced those elements he found attractive, promptly discarding the rest. To dismiss the notion of papal infallibility, however, does not necessarily imply a lack of respect or admiration for the Pope. Indeed, Jack travelled to the Vatican at Easter 1965 and was very anxious to see his spiritual leader, Pope Paul VI. The Pope had been washing the feet of some handicapped people on Maundy Thursday in the Lateran Church. Although again unimpressed by the lavish ceremonial, when the Pope eventually did emerge to be received by the crowds, Preger found himself swept along by the power and emotion of the occasion. While large numbers of Romans waved their handkerchiefs as a sign of friendship towards their leader, and organ music from the smaller churches filled the air with spirituality and love, Jack knew that he had found a new home.

Of course Jack Preger is not the first Jew to convert to Catholicism. Many have embarked on a similar course, among them the present Archbishop of Paris, His Eminence Jean-Marie Lustiger. Preger might not be the stuff of which prospective archbishops are made, but by the time of his confirmation he had indeed journeyed some way from those early days at the Manchester Yeshiva. There, several teachers had high hopes that the bright, questioning young boy might one day graduate from rabbinical college, and that he might in time take their ancient teachings back to the Jewish community.

He had left behind those Oxford days too, when he had been pleased to ape a Catholic priest for no other reason than that it had struck him as a most preposterous thing to do at the time. Preger might not have emerged as a devout Catholic in the traditional mould, but the religion was certainly no longer the raw material for cheap laughs.

Jack Preger had received a message. The words 'Become a doctor' had entered his head within a matter of seconds. By contrast, to become a doctor would take several years of study. And what of Gernos Farm? While it was more than clear that Jack's role in life was no longer to toil alone on a remote farm in Wales, it was just not possible to simply walk away from such a massive undertaking. How then to implement this weighty injunction from the Almighty?

6
Doctor Jack

Preger's letters of application to the various medical schools of the United Kingdom had met with little success. The best response was from Sheffield University, whose tutor of admissions was particularly sympathetic to mature students. It was indeed an offer, but only to add Jack to the faculty's long waiting list of applicants. Every other institution required a minimum of three Advanced Level passes in science, with respectable grades. Nobody denied that Jack's academic record was impressive. But since it was firmly rooted in the liberal arts it was seen, not unreasonably perhaps, as entirely irrelevant to the study of modern medicine. A second-class degree in philosophy, politics and economics from however august an institution, left virtually everyone he applied to singularly unmoved. Preger read the writing on the wall. It was not a particularly pleasant message: that before proceeding any further he would have to arm himself with qualifications in subjects happily abandoned many years ago. It was time to unravel the mysteries of chemistry, physics and biology.

Jack therefore enrolled at Swansea College of Further Education. However, having done manual work for thirteen years, he soon realized that here was a battle in which victory was by no means guaranteed. Nor did his personal circumstances smooth the difficult transition to full-time study. Obliged to return to Gernos every weekend in order to monitor conditions on the farm, Jack spent as much time grappling with the udders of his cows as with the principles of science. Milking was an unavoidable but extremely time-consuming process that he was obliged to perform at least twice before setting off for Swansea again. While the experience might be said to constitute practical biology, it bore little relation to the syllabus.

Although Jack at first considered himself fortunate to have found a married couple whom he paid to live in and work on the farm during the week, it soon became apparent that it was not a satisfactory arrangement. Moreover, exhausted by the perpetual shuttle between Swansea and Gernos, he found himself unable to keep up with his studies. Desperate to succeed despite the mounting odds against him, it was on returning to Gernos one weekend that Jack realized that a rather strange notion had entered his head:

I used to have all these sheep on the cliffs on the rough grazing land and I'd go up to see how they were. Once in every ten years or so you could see right across to the Wicklow Mountains in Ireland. They had been visible on one occasion during the summer of 1958, when there had been this really ultra-clear day, but unfortunately I had missed them. I'd never seen these hills, so they really didn't mean anything. But I got what I guess you have to call an obsession. I would often go off towards these cliffs to see if I might be able to view the Wicklow Mountains. And I came to the rather peculiar conclusion that things would somehow never work out for me — in terms of selling the farm or qualifying as a doctor — unless and until I had seen Ireland. One weekend both Cathy and Justice had been staying with me at Gernos. We took Justice back to Fishguard, from where he was going to catch the boat-train back to London. It was a most beautiful day and there was a boat tied up there. Since I had this married couple staying on the farm I rang them and announced that I was off to Ireland for a couple of days — just impromptu like that. We had very little money with us, so Cathy and I hitched a lift to Dublin, where we slept in a barn just outside the city.

Perhaps Jack's compulsive desire to view Irish soil was not as fanciful or far-fetched as it might seem. The visit to Dublin was to be something of a watershed. Jack had already applied to study medicine at the city's Trinity College, but the college's response, by even the most generous of interpretations, had been lukewarm. Jack decided that a personal appearance might enhance his prospects, but he was rapidly disabused of such a notion. For this time Trinity's message was more forthright: his case was hopeless; he had no chance whatsoever of gaining a place.

Jack was about to leave the building when a voice from the admissions office casually ventured an alternative suggestion, as if to cushion the blow:

'You might try the Royal College of Surgeons, though.'

It was particularly good advice, as Jack recalls with some delight:

I hadn't applied to the College of Surgeons, but I went there immediately. The girl in the office listened to me quite carefully. It turned out that she was married to an English chap who was himself a medical student in the college. The fact that he too was a bit older than the usual run of students was one thing, and another link was that I was English and there weren't that many Englishmen in Dublin in those days. She went into the Registrar's office and told him to give me a place immediately, which he did on that very same day. The fantastic thing about this offer was that it was not subject to my 'A' level results – which, looking at it realistically, I don't suppose I ever would have got. All they were concerned about at Surgeons was that I should complete their pre-med year, which provided another year's fees for very little additional expenditure. And since rumour had it that the pre-med year was a good deal easier than the dreaded 'A' levels, I was absolutely thrilled. I went back to my chemistry tutor in Swansea, who was a real dragon, and informed her that I would have to concentrate on selling the farm because I had been offered this place in medical school for the October of 1965.

Selling the farm was easier said than done. It was not at all unknown for properties such as Gernos to remain on the market for the best part of a decade. Aware that it would not be easy, Jack purchased and put aside one firkin of beer, the consumption of which was to take place only when the legal title of the property had been properly conveyed into the hands of a new owner.

But then the intervention of a most unlikely third party swayed the balance decisively in Jack's favour. Idi Amin, the Ugandan dictator, was in the throes of summarily expelling both English and Asian farmers from the protectorate recently relinquished by the British, and thus from lands that were rightfully theirs. Jack's radical credentials were not much tested during his time at Gernos, but, ironically, the consequences of this present flagrant abuse of human rights served his interests rather well. Now, far from being unable to dispose of the farm, there were two cash buyers anxious to acquire its vast estate, their common enthusiasm to do so conveniently pushing up the price all the while. By a further strange twist Gernos was eventually sold to a couple who were retiring from practising medicine in the Third World to take up farming in Wales. Jack was delighted finally to have disposed of Gernos, and recalls thus his last days in that remote spot:

Whilst I had found a buyer for the farm I still had to sell all the stock and the machines. But after the sale was agreed I thought that we had all worked very hard and the time had come to get our hands on that beer. Dai was back with me by this stage and it turned out that he had already got his hands on it. The farmers who bought our machinery knew that Dai was working on the farm and naturally assumed that he was *compos mentis*. One of these farmers who had purchased a tractor asked Dai if he would get it up to the road for him. Dai could manage a tractor – but not drunk. Notwithstanding his state of inebriation, Dai leaped onto the machine, drove it straight off the road and into a tree. It wasn't quite the finale I had envisaged at Gernos – because we had to ask all the farmers who had bought other items of stock or machinery to come and help us pull the wretched thing out of the tree!

And what of Maritta's share of the proceeds? All she had received to date was one unannounced visit from her estranged husband's young lover, followed soon after by an unsolicited and rather insolent letter. It was understandable that Maritta should want to benefit from the sale of the farm, for it was with her money that Gernos had been purchased. Yet it was Jack who had toiled the land. An agreement was reached, though only after the exchange of a number of solicitors' letters. Jack was to receive the proceeds of the sale of the stock, the crops and the machinery in addition to a share of the farm's sale price. Not surprisingly, the extent of that share was disputed and the source of some acrimony, provoking a further round of carefully drafted legal correspondence.

Eventually Jack emerged with enough money to buy a house in Dublin. It was his intention to convert the property into a number of flats that, it was hoped, would not only generate an income but also finance his studies. It was a return to the world of property speculation, to which he had first been introduced by Maritta over a decade ago. The only difference was that this time he would be without her formidable flair for both commerce and design. And, as Jack was soon to discover, in terms of property development London and Dublin were worlds apart.

To sell Gernos had been the right thing to do. Nor was there any question about Jack's fierce determination to qualify as a doctor. The message he had so mysteriously received had not simply vanished overnight. One other thing was certain: his marriage to Maritta was effectively at an end, even if the law had still to catch up with that sad reality. But what of Cathy? Was Jack as certain about the future of this relationship as he was about these other issues? True, they would be together from time to time during his pre-med year in Dublin. But Cathy knew very well that Jack's mind was far from made up, as she remembers with some sorrow:

Jack and I were very fond of one another for a very long time. I never lived with Jack as such, because he kept changing his mind about marrying me. He was constantly on and off about the whole thing. I was looking for a commitment in the relationship, and in the end I met and married another man, Tony Bentley, although he too turned out to be totally unsuitable.

For eight years there was no contact between Cathy and Jack. When eventually they met again, Cathy was the mother of three children and, like Jack, a divorcee. Maritta and Jack were divorced on 14 April 1967, the decree absolute coinciding with Alun's seventh birthday. It was some eighteen months since father and son had set eyes on one another, but this was only the beginning of a much longer separation. It took several more years for Jack's annulment to come through, and then only thanks to the intervention of a new and more liberal Archbishop of Dublin.

Jack soon discovered that the Royal College of Surgeons could justifiably boast a long history of internationalism. In 1962, of the 700 or so students in the medical school, only 10 per cent were Irish nationals, an average of just a dozen students per academic year. In the mid-sixties, however, the Council of the Royal College adopted the 'one-thirds rule': one third of prospective students were to be Irish, one third from the developed world, and the remaining third from the developing world. It was a formula based on a not unreasonable assumption: that the college, being an Irish medical school, required at the very least a representative core of Irish students. But it would be some time before the Royal College would be able to send out Irish doctors to attend to the requirements of Irish people. For of those students graduating between 1964 and 1973, while there were indeed 125 Irish doctors emerging from the Faculty, there were 167 from South Africa, and many others from a wide range of remote and underdeveloped countries including Ethiopia, Malawi, Sierra Leone, Tanganyika and Zanzibar.

Whatever its composition, Jack was a happy man at the Royal College. No more depression now. Whereas at Oxford he had needed time to find his feet, 'Surgeons' appeared to demand little adjustment. In a letter to Father Cunnane, Jack could scarcely contain his enthusiasm. Here was a new man speaking:

Dublin is great, I really love it. I'm sleeping in the room George Bernard Shaw was born in at 22 Synge Street. Let's hope my handwriting improves with all the literary vibrations in the air.

Thank you for all your help, instruction and otherwise. I feel about half my age nowadays!

And there appeared to be little danger of Jack's *joie de vivre* suddenly petering out. Every potential obstacle to his quest for fulfilment appeared to have been removed to his entire satisfaction. Two months later he wrote again to the Catholic priest:

The programme here is a pretty full one, to put it mildly. And correspondence fairly piles up, as does the homework. But Dublin seems more and more attractive. Surgeons is a very cosmopolitan College and the atmosphere is so friendly.

The pre-med year in Dublin might well have been easier than sitting 'A' levels in Swansea, but it was by no means plain sailing. Nor was it possible to miraculously bypass physics, chemistry and biology. Jack's chemistry teacher in Dublin was adamant that students must obtain a real understanding of the subject. Whereas at Oxford Jack had been able to discard certain philosophical concepts that he found uninviting or just plain unintelligible, it was simply not possible to do likewise with the sciences. He could not simply brush aside the more taxing parts of the syllabus. Of course the chemistry teacher's reasoning was entirely sound: an all-round understanding of the subject would be an essential part of a doctor's armoury during his or her career, particularly when it came to prescribing medication. Jack failed the chemistry examination, but scraped through on the retake. Since he was scarcely able to comprehend the theoretical side of the subject, it was a thoroughly dispiriting experience, a far cry from the days of Stand Grammar, where he had performed so well.

The following year Jack continued to battle hard, this time with the allied subject of biochemistry, and was once again obliged to repeat the exam. Unlike many students from overseas, especially those of Asian origin (many of whom appeared able to recite entire pages of medical texts parrot-fashion) Jack found great difficulty in absorbing and retaining material. And if the odd sympathetic professor had not been to hand, he would have been in the very deepest of water. So it was particularly timely that he happened to do sufficiently well in the physiology examinations for his professor in that subject to be able to persuade a colleague in anatomy to transfer some marks from one subject to the other, a highly unorthodox procedure. Jack's place at Surgeons was precarious indeed.

Nor were matters helped by the arrival of a most unexpected visitor: an emissary despatched from Cardigan, whose journey had been wholly funded by Father Cunnane. His brief had been quite simple and clear-cut: to track down a struggling student by the name of Preger. The surprised student wasted no time at all in writing to the priest in order to formally lodge his complaint:

> Last Monday I looked up during a break in one of the lectures and groaned as an all too familiar (bearded) figure hovered in the doorway. John had crossed swords with one of the College porters but, inevitably, had run me to earth finally. When I found who had financed the venture I thought it was all some horrible practical joke . . .

'John' was in fact Dai Clarke, whose parting gift to Preger at Gernos had been to launch an unprovoked attack on a tree while precariously perched on a tractor. His arrival in Dublin happened to coincide with Jack's purchase of a house in the south of the city. It had been especially selected by Jack with a view to conversion into small flats. Although Dai protested loudly at being set to work so soon after his arrival, it was an arrangement that would work to their mutual advantage, albeit for a limited period of time.

The property was a three-storey house situated at 14 Windsor Road, and Dai set about the labouring with characteristic gusto. But he set about the consumption of large quantities of alcohol with even greater enthusiasm, a project that culminated in his arrest by the Irish Garda for the offence of loitering with intent. Although Jack bailed him out in respect of that particular offence, Dai moved on again, this time losing contact for good. It was the end of a bizarre relationship between two men whose backgrounds could scarcely have been more different: one a drunken tramp, the other an Oxford graduate. Yet each had somehow come to depend on the other at various stages of their lives.

Jack might not have accepted every single tenet of the Catholic faith, but there was no doubting the depth or sincerity of his religious convictions. Indeed, it was to the power of faith and healing, rather than to the conventional medicine of his studies, that Jack turned when, during the pre-med year, he encountered difficulties with his eyesight. Perhaps it was the greatly increased reading that had taxed his eyes so. Whatever its origin, the problem became so acute that at one stage he could hardly read at all. Instead of heading to Dublin's long-established departments of ophthalmology and optics, as might have been expected of a student of medicine, it was to an isolated well near Waterford that Jack turned for help. It was said that St Declan's well could perform miracles, as Jack explains:

One man was so grateful for the improvement in his wife's sight that he wanted to do something to improve the well, which he did by laying some rather grotesque concrete all over the beautiful surrounding countryside and building an incredible chapel, which looks more like a greenhouse gone wrong. I went down there in desperation, I suppose. In fact I went there three times, because that's the amount of times you are supposed to go. You're also supposed to go for Mass on one day during the year called St Declan's Day, when a Mass is held at the well. I used to take the well water back to Dublin and bathe my eyes with it. I won't say that there was a miraculous cure, but I did manage to start reading again and pass my examinations. I would always keep this bottle of water with me and it was out of gratitude to St Declan, I guess, that I took on the middle name of Declan, which now appears on my official baptismal certificate.

Jack attended Mass not just during times of need, but throughout his time at Surgeons. He was as good a Catholic as any other Dubliner. But that did not deter one particular character, one of Jack's tenants in Windsor Road, from classifying his landlord as Jewish. To this individual, there was simply no doubt about

Preger's pedigree: he was a Jew. His supposition was not without a certain logic: the surname had a distinctly European-Jewish flavour, and there could surely be no mistaking Preger's Jewish looks. This was considered by the tenant to be sufficient justification for making a series of anti-Semitic remarks, although he could not muster sufficient courage to address them to Jack's face. This troublesome tenant must surely have ended up wondering if he might not after all have come to the wrong conclusion about Jack's Jewishness. Because when a Catholic priest later came to bless the house in Windsor Road, at Jack's request, the most confused expression in the house belonged to this disgruntled character, the only anti-Semite Jack ever encountered in eight years in Ireland.

As if there were not already enough demands on Jack's time, he decided to launch himself into the world of sport. Still heavy around the shoulders from the days of Gernos, he could do more than merely hold his own on the rugby field. Neither his size nor his weight, however, spared him from a series of injuries, as he would complain in a letter to Father Cunnane:

> I've taken up rugby in a mild way and so far have only had my head forced between my shoulders, my thumb sprained so it ballooned up grotesquely, and some chest muscles sufficiently strained to require physiotherapy. Incredibly, I feel fine on it all. But the most exhausting of all was my first Irish dance – a bit like Cardigan Mart on a wet, crowded day.

But it was on the hockey field that Jack would really earn his colours. Although he had taken up the sport from scratch, he soon earned a place in the Royal College of Surgeons' first team; no mean achievement since matches were played under the auspices of the Republic of Ireland's junior league. Competition for a place was fierce, especially from the East African Asians, and at one stage Jack's was the only white face in the entire team.

Study, speculation, spirituality and now sport. Was there time for anything else? Yes indeed. For Jack also became very involved in one of the undisputed highlights of the academic year at Surgeons, the Christmas review. It might not have been on a par with the Cambridge Footlights, but it enjoyed a formidable reputation all the same, with hundreds of people cramming into the hall and many others being turned back at the doors. Before long Jack was writing the entire show. Skilled with his pen, incisive with his wit, Jack found that his talents as a scriptwriter were much in demand:

> It was incredible fun writing all this garbage. We had some pretty good actors and actresses too. We would just pull to bits everything that went on in the hospital. Don't forget that the consultants were virtually considered to be Gods, but woe betide them if they had anything wrong with them – twitches, limps. I couldn't believe what the directors could make of all the rubbish I was churning out. Everyone was involved – porters, nursing staff and so on.

What of Jack's long-standing tendency to manic depression? It was certainly not much in evidence during his years at Surgeons. Or rather it was contained within bounds, the key to coping with the disorder. In fact the manic behaviour was never far from the surface:

> A month or so before that Christmas review I wouldn't do any studying at all. I'd sit there with a writing pad and start working immediately after I'd had my high tea at about six-thirty or seven. I wouldn't have any ideas at all to begin with, but I'd force myself to write a sketch. By about eleven I'd be jumping with all these characters and couldn't get them down onto paper fast enough. By midnight it would all be over, but of course I couldn't get to sleep. So I'd read through the whole thing again, correcting and amending as necessary. By one in the morning I was again full of this creativity, and it was quite impossible for me to switch off, even though I knew I had to go to college the next day, or rather later that morning. But sometimes this would frighten me, because I was aware that it could all get out of control. It had done so before at Oxford, and I knew very well that it could do so again.

It was fortunate for Jack that in Dublin at least, his illness never got out of control. On the contrary, he was experiencing at Surgeons greater enjoyment of life than at any other time he could recall. But what kind of doctor did Jack aspire to be? A cosy general practitioner serving the Jewish community of Manchester, so familiar from the days of his childhood? Or with a practice in rural Wales, attuned to the requirements of the agricultural and farming communities? He found both propositions equally unattractive. Because, from the outset, there was no doubt at all in Jack's mind about why he had embarked on a career in medicine. It was for one precise purpose. Cathy had described it rather succinctly in her letter to Maritta: Jack was 'dazzled by the great good he can do as a doctor'. But where was the stage on which this great good was to be acted out? In the Third World, of course.

Not that Surgeons suffered from any shortage of students from the underdeveloped countries. Indeed, in Jack's year there were 111 students from thirty-three different nations. Did the majority of these prospective doctors from overseas share his enthusiasm for providing medicine to less fortunate groups in their own countries?

I wouldn't exactly preach to these students from Africa or Asia. I would just ask what they would be up to when they went back home. Actually a lot of them weren't intending to go home at all, but were heading for the United States with every intention of remaining there. I gave up in the end because I realized that we were on completely different wavelengths. In fact I used to watch their faces glaze over when we talked about issues of development and Third World medicine – it was obviously painful for them to have to listen to me drone on. The truth was that I was becoming a kind of development bore and so I eventually learned to just let the subject drop.

Whenever a legitimate forum presented itself, however, Jack would not hesitate to speak his mind. In what was by far the longest single entry in the *Students' Yearbook* for 1971, Jack could scarcely conceal his enthusiasm for the challenges that lay ahead:

In saying farewell to so many good friends of so many years' standing, I hope I may be forgiven for emphasizing at this stage how important it is to work out for ourselves what matters most. It is, I believe, the patient who comes first: his interests and wellbeing. The greater his needs, the more we should be concerned with him; irrespective of his ability to pay. All this is obvious and for that reason far too easily lost sight of. Within the limits of our family commitments, I feel we should endeavour to work at least for a few years in those developing countries in which there is such a shortage of medical personnel. There is an undeniable risk to personal safety in some of these countries but stable regimes can be found.

For Jack, the most important question had become that of tactics and timing. The issue was not whether or not he was Third World bound, but precisely where to, and when. Jack approached the professor of vascular surgery for advice. Professor McGowan was something of a rarity at Surgeons, a medic who had practical experience of working in underdeveloped countries. In his eagerness to help those normally deprived of adequate medical provision, Jack was anxious to establish exactly where his intern year would most usefully be spent. McGowan's advice was unambiguous: he should remain in Ireland. The professor pointed out that while he would be most unlikely to encounter any tropical diseases in Dublin, the underlying pathologies of other illnesses with which he was bound to have contact would not be unrelated.

As if foreshadowing the great role he had in mind for himself, Jack then sought another opinion. He wrote to Albert Schweitzer, the celebrated German mission doctor who had received the Nobel Peace Prize in 1952 for teaching 'reverence for life', in order to be sure that McGowan's advice was sound. Schweitzer was working in the Belgian Congo, where he had established a colony for lepers. His opinion concurred with the professor's: that the intern year would indeed be best spent in Ireland. Jack was at last convinced that he should postpone setting off for a year.

Desperate as he was to venture forth into the Third World, Jack would not have been the first of the three Preger children to have done so. Both Leslie and Anita had already beaten him to it. Disenchanted with life as a general practitioner in the Midlands, Leslie had responded to an advertisement placed by a German doctor for assistance in his practice in Calcutta. Since Anita was suffering from a medical condition that invariably improved in a warm climate, she had decided to accompany her brother and keep house. Nor was Jack the first Preger eager to do something to alleviate the plight of the poor, as Leslie points out:

I was working in Calcutta whilst Jackie was sampling various types of chocolates with Attwood Statistics and then, later, when he was farming in Wales. I used to give a certain amount of my time – about fifteen per cent of it I think – to helping poor families. I worked as a GP in Calcutta from 1955 to 1959 and it used to be a pretty pleasant life out there for us in those days. There was another doctor working in a neighbouring practice who had written a book called *Medicine, my Passport*. I showed this book to my brother and I think it had an influence on him. Although Jackie didn't envy me in any way I think he realized that medicine at least enabled you to break out of the mould in which you found yourself, and to broaden your horizons.

Perhaps it was because he felt particularly protective towards his younger brother that Leslie was not at all enthusiastic about Jack's following in his footsteps by working overseas. Leslie impressed on him that should he ignore this advice and pursue his ambitious projects, there were two qualities that were bound to be called on time and again: toughness and determination. And that a double dose would be required should he ever work in Bengal.

It was as well that Jack was showing signs of both qualities. Although a new intern at St Laurence's Hospital in Dublin, he was beginning to cut his Third World teeth. A particularly officious administrator at the hospital, known as 'Mothballs Dawson', helped Jack with this toughening-up process. Mothballs took such a dim view of interns in general that he found himself quite unable to refer to them as doctors, even though it was a title that had been hard earned. He preferred to dub all interns 'juniors', as if to remind them of their lowly rank within the rigid hierarchy of the hospital's administration. The very junior and newly qualified Dr Jack Preger was working on the neurosurgical ward and, like all interns, found the work gruelling in the extreme. Experience on the wards convinced Jack that a telephone was essential for the satisfactory performance of his duties. It came as no surprise to him to learn that Mothballs did not share this view:

Old Mothballs was opposed to just about everything we did. He thought that a bleep was good enough for the likes of us, but it wasn't. Because every time it went off it would wake you up, and you'd then have to run halfway round the doctors' residence to find a phone in a passageway. You then had to try to find out what had happened, and where you were required. It might have been in intensive care, casualty, or any one of a number of other wards. And there was no one else between us interns and the consultant neurosurgeon. There was one occasion on which a senior house officer had been called under such circumstances and by the time he had woken up and run to the phone – down the stairs, across the road, through the entrances and passageways and finally upstairs to the patient – well, the poor chap was dead. I said to Mothballs that I really didn't think that I could manage the job safely without a phone. He quickly produced his reply:

'Well, that's up to you, isn't it.'

I gave as good as I got, replying that I was going to resign. Well, he thought that he'd got me into this corner from which I'd come crawling out, because you can imagine that interns just don't resign, not after all that study. A day or so passed and he called me in and asked what I was going to do. I said that I was resigning and was about to hand in my letter of resignation. I think that Mothballs must have got frightened. Because when I got back to the doctors' residence, the lady who was running it said:

'That's strange, Dr Preger – Dawson has just reallocated you to a ground-floor registrar's room with running hot and cold water and a telephone.'

Gaining a room with a telephone might not have been a major victory. But it was the first display of Jack's fighting spirit, a resource to which he would later turn time and time again.

Jack completed his intern year at St Laurence's in 1972. It was the culmination of seven years' hard work, and since Jack was a most unlikely student of medicine, the odds against his succeeding had seemed formidable. And yet, now forty-two, he was not all that proud to have completed the course:

> The awful thing is that once you have done your intern year you realize that you really don't know anything at all, and that you should be doing all these postgraduate courses. Because it takes years to understand the limitations of your own knowledge. I also realized that I had a great deal to learn from the nurses on the wards – experience which they had acquired over the years from working away both day and night.

Bertha Preger was considerably less restrained about her son's success. Having left The Danes during the course of the previous year, she had become increasingly depressed and isolated. Now in her early seventies and living alone in Southport, she could surely have received no better tonic than Jack's telephone call from Ireland bearing the good news. Now Bertha could say with pride: 'My sons, the doctors.' It might have been said half jokingly, but it seldom failed to impress her Jewish contemporaries.

What failed to impress both Bertha and her friends, though, was what Jack intended to do with his newly acquired qualification. The general consensus appeared to be that going overseas somehow made it all a waste of time. Jack's mind was made up, though; it had been for several years. What he had not yet decided was where to go. One possibility had been to go to work in Jamaica, but the necessary arrangements had proved extraordinarily complex. And then, one lunchtime, in the doctors' modest residence, Jack happened to be listening to Radio Eireann. An appeal was being broadcast on behalf of Concern, a Dublin-based charity involved in development and reconstruction. Concern was very eager to recruit doctors and nurses to carry out relief work in Bangladesh, a country desperate for emergency medical assistance and advice after suffering the ravages of a bitter war.

And I decided to go. It was not as if Bangladesh was in my blood or a lifetime's aim. It was just a spur-of-the-moment thing. But I did feel that this was the sort of thing I wanted to do. I didn't really know anything about Bangladesh or its history. In fact, to be honest, I didn't even know where it was.

Leslie Preger knew all about Bangladesh, though. Having worked in Bengal for three years, he was vigorously opposed to his younger brother accepting such a vague and poorly paid posting. Antipathetic to the Bengalis, Leslie was convinced that Jack's work would be a waste of both time and energy. He had seen it all before. So eager was he to dissuade his brother from going that he offered to pay for an airline ticket to any destination in the world other than Bengal. It was a bribe that failed to sway Jack. Leslie responded by offering an even larger sum of money with which Jack might establish himself in medical practice elsewhere in the world. But there was no stopping Jack now. Having accepted the job with Concern, he turned out to be the only doctor in the whole of Ireland to have responded to its appeal. An inauspicious start perhaps, and, looking back, Jack concedes:

'It was only upon arriving in Bangladesh that I realized why my brother had been so desperate to stop me from ever setting foot in Bengal.'

7

For Sale: Babies from Bangladesh

Having arrived in Bangladesh in the summer of 1972, Jack began to reflect on the numerous challenges facing him. The situation in that country was desperate indeed. Only one year earlier Bangladesh had been officially East Pakistan. Despite the fact that Bangladesh was separated from the other five provinces of Pakistan by well over a thousand miles of Indian territory, the notion of a bipartite Pakistan had been hurriedly devised by the British as the days of the Raj drew to a close. East Pakistan had long been the poor relation of West Pakistan, a situation that had fuelled the independence movement. The price of the creation of this fledgling state, however, had been high. Independence had been achieved, but only after a bitter and bloody civil war in which three million people lost their lives.

Another consequence of the Bangladeshis' yearning for sovereignty was that at least ten million refugees had been created, most of whom had crossed the border and made their way to India. The war had brought even more chaos to a country still reeling from the effects of a disastrous cyclone and tidal wave that had ravaged a vast area of the Ganges River delta, leaving almost a quarter of a million dead. Bangladesh was in every possible way a disaster area. It was against this background of havoc and despair that Jack Preger, medical practitioner, had set out for Dacca, the capital of this new and troubled land.

Not surprisingly it was not long before Jack's eyes were opened to the reality of life in the Third World. It was grim. Only now did he begin to grasp the seriousness of his brother's warning. As for his posting with Concern, it came to an abrupt end before it had really got under way, as Jack explained in a letter to Father Cunnane. It would surely have brought a wry smile to Leslie's lips:

> Your reference for me to Concern must have been great – only I resigned after 2.5 weeks here. Then jobless for six weeks. You cannot conceive of the set-up: the corruption, inhumanity, indifference and needless suffering. No one gives a hang about medical care really – not with seventy-five million on fifty-five thousand square miles. And ten thousand more babies daily. The work is interesting and the tropical cases fascinating. But the shortage of drugs is beyond belief. Due in part to Government hoarding and widespread pilfering and misappropriation. I've been working in the camps in my spare time from the Children's Hospital, but it's pathetic how little one can achieve when there's no backing from any organization.

The training in the principles of medicine offered by the Royal College of Surgeons had been first-class. But no course of study could have prepared Jack for the horrors and hopelessness of Bangladesh. Not that it was his inclination to cut and run. On the contrary, for he embarked on a schedule of work that made the rigorous regime of his internship at St Laurence's Hospital look like child's play. For twenty-four hours a day, seven days a week, Jack was on call. After working in the children's hospital in the morning, he would transfer to the camps in the afternoon. In the evening he would return to the children's hospital, where, more often than not, he would attempt to smuggle in some of the more troubling cases from the camps. He attended regularly to patients suffering from both malnutrition and dysentery, and discovered that it was commonplace for five children to die in a single night, causing five mothers to pace the wards screaming with the raw agony of grief. Occasionally an English or Irish nurse was brought in to help run the hospital, but every single nurse with whom Jack worked suffered from a mental breakdown of some description. Unable to cope with the nightmare being acted out before their eyes, they eventually became unavailable for work. In conditions reminiscent of the Dark Ages, Jack would battle on, often alone, at times stitching up a woman after childbirth with nothing but a hurricane lamp to guide his hand.

The camps were for refugees, of course, but for a particular type of refugee: the Biharis. The Bihari people had emigrated from India to East Bengal throughout almost two centuries. Some had journeyed from the province of Bihar, others from what was once called the United Province. Two things distinguish them from the majority of Bangladeshis: the fact that their mother tongue is Urdu rather than Bengali, and, more importantly, their support for the defeated armies of West Pakistan during the civil war. Having made the mistake of backing the losing side, they were being treated as enemy aliens. This blatant persecution of the Biharis Jack found himself unable and unwilling to accept:

It is really difficult to describe the conditions of those camps, because they were so utterly horrific. About eighty thousand people were living in total squalor, dying like dogs – with TB, smallpox, dysentery and scabies everywhere you looked. The trouble was that the hospitals didn't want these people because they were Biharis. It just amazed me what the Bengalis could do to these people, who, after all, are fellow-Muslims. Because they had supported West Pakistan they were referred to as 'stranded Pakistanis', or 'non-locals' was another euphemism, and they had to suffer a kind of collective punishment imposed on them by the Bengalis. On top of all this there was such corruption and mismanagement in the camps, such indifference in government offices, such an appalling attitude on the part of politicians, that I really had a hard time working in Bangladesh and absorbing all that was going on.

Jack had been in Bangladesh some six weeks before learning of the plight of the Biharis. It was during a tour of one of the camps that he suddenly found himself, like the nurses before him, unable to bear any longer the severity and scale of the human suffering. Jack suddenly broke down in tears. Because the excursion around the camp was being conducted in torrential rain, those escorting him failed to notice that Jack was crying from the very depths of his soul. It was the plight of the Bihari children in particular that had cut a swathe through his last emotional defences.

> That outburst was all over in fifteen minutes. I kept on walking round the camp when I suddenly found that my emotions had got the better of me, and there was no stopping the tears. It was a pathetic sight: hundreds of children lined up in all this terrible mud and raw sewage in the pouring rain of the monsoon, getting a glass of milk a day if they were lucky. But as I cried I realized that this was the work I had to do.

It was true that Jack's heart went out to the Bihari children. But those tears were as much for the suffering inflicted on the Jews as they were for the Bihari refugees. True, Jack had converted to Catholicism and several years had elapsed since he was baptized and confirmed. Yet it was the discarded faith of his forebears that had prompted his emotional release. The parallels between the plight of the Biharis and the persecution of European Jewry by the Nazis were so startling that neither Jew nor gentile could fail to notice them. Certainly there was no doubt in Jack's mind:

> I remember the thought that 'here are the Jews of Bangladesh' coming into my mind as soon as I entered those camps. The Biharis were being singled out because they happened to belong to this community. Children who hadn't even been conceived at the time of fighting were being punished along with all the rest. The new-born would die of tetanus. Their mothers would have no milk for them and many would just waste away in their early years. Others would get smallpox or, more likely, TB, which was like a plague there, with the most incredible death rates that you can imagine. The Biharis were herded into about sixty-six camps and women who had played no part in the fighting at all likewise had to die terrible deaths. Every now and then the army would go

in and inflict the most severe punishments on them. It was just like the ghettoes of Russia and Poland where there would be the occasional pogrom. Of course it wasn't on the same scale as the Holocaust, and it has to be said that members of this minority group did do terrible things to the Bengalis in the war. But it was the issue of collective guilt which struck a chord with me in terms of the parallels with European Jewry. Thoughts of Auschwitz, Bergen-Belsen and Buchenwald were never far from my mind. In Manchester immediately after the war, I'd seen the state of those Jews who came out of the concentration camps, and I felt I really had no choice other than to speak up for the cause of the Biharis.

If this represented a shift away from a strictly medical role, towards the volatile and violent world of the politics of Bangladesh, it was a transition Jack made without any overt agonizing. For him, it was simply the most natural thing to do. The radical politics of Jack Preger, last seen during his Oxford years, had resurfaced.

One of Jack's more mundane duties while working in Bangladesh was the compilation of statistics. Some of the techniques he had learnt twenty years earlier in market research were called into play once again, but now the agenda was radically different. For it became Jack's task to document mortality rates among refugees. There was one particularly large clinic in Saidpur, in the north-west of Bangladesh, where an entire town of Biharis was to be found. Seldom was there any doubt about the cause of death. The figures told a tragic tale: so many thousands had died of TB; so many thousands had died of starvation. Yet the Bangladesh Red Cross began to reject statistical data painstakingly prepared by Preger. It seemed that the doctor's terminology was not to their taste. The word 'starvation' was no longer to be employed, and the more politically acceptable 'malnutrition' was to be used in its place. Jack was not prepared to play ball, and it was not long before he was at loggerheads with the authorities.

For Jack, there could be no cover-up. On the contrary, he now sought to tell of the human suffering masked by those anonymous statistics. Always skilled with the written word, and now fuelled by anger, he began to draft reports, which he would send to anyone who showed an interest in the plight of the Biharis. The achievement of publicity in the West by a doctor working in the East was by no means easy, but the London-based Minority Rights Group finally gave Jack a hearing. Aware that it would not be in his interests to disclose his true identity, he had entitled the document: *The Situation in the Bihari Camps – by a Doctor working in Bangladesh*. Anonymous though it was, there was no mistaking its message to the world.

It is difficult to imagine how it can be possible for the Commonwealth nations to allow such monstrosities to continue to exist in a Commonwealth country. In spite of all efforts by the voluntary agencies, who have replaced the International Committee of the Red Cross and the Bangladesh Red Cross in the camps, conditions remain unbelievably bad. In Geneva camp two-thirds of the huts still need repair, latrines are broken and the water supply is unhygienic. The population of the camp is stated to be 38,740. In Borga the huts are collapsing and there is no apparent means of draining for the camp sewage. At Rangpur the Biharis have been evicted from the warehouse they were sheltering in and the re-formed Ispahanic camp No. 3 has serious housing and sanitation problems. In Bansbar camp at Saidpur there are still sick, malnourished children in evidence, in spite of all the medical work in the town.

Since he was subjected to a daily dose of cases of malpractice and malnutrition, it was hardly surprising that Jack's nights were also disturbed. He grew unable to abruptly switch off from the squalor of the camps, and images of dead or dying children would flash through his mind. The overwrought doctor found some solace in Thomas Hardy; the English novelist's style was so evocative that a few pages from *Tess of the D'Urbervilles* would produce soothing images in his mind, allowing sleep to come, at least until the next call. There was also a more immediate source from whom Jack was able to draw both courage and inspiration: Mother Teresa. Her Missionary of Charity nuns had been running a feeding programme in Old Dacca and she had come to inspect it. Jack wrote to his friend the priest to explain the impact her visit to Bangladesh had made on him:

> When she left I had the most extraordinary feeling. I have just seen a recent copy of *Time* which quotes Muggeridge on exactly the same feeling. I believe that she and her nuns have hold of an absolute mystical truth and the longer I work here the more apparent does this become.

Individuals might have impressed Jack; organizations did not. While he retained a firm commitment to the Catholic faith, he did not feel the same about the Catholic Church in Bengal. For him, its silence concerning the plight of the Bihari refugees was wholly contemptible. The theology was sound enough. But where in practical terms was the evidence of the message and teachings of Jesus Christ? As Jack later wrote:

> I recall working in the Dacca Bihari refugee camps in 1972, and catching a glimpse one Sunday morning of the congregation coming out of the Catholic cathedral. I could not believe that degradation on the scale of the Bihari camps at that time could exist in the same city as that beautifully dressed and well-nourished Catholic congregation, indulging in social intercourse at their leisure after Mass.

That was the polite way of putting the matter, in language acceptable to readers of the Catholic magazine *The Tablet*, to which Jack became an occasional contributor. He masked the fury that lay behind his disenchantment with the Catholic authorities in Bengal. But face to face his language was rather different:

> I would tell the organization that I worked for what a pack of bastards they were. They were stuffing themselves in a nice residential area of Dacca, and people were dying like dogs just down the road. The Biharis were being eaten alive by scabies, which often would become infected and cover the victims in abscesses. I remember going up to one particular Catholic priest

to ask him for some soap. The idea was to let the refugees wash prior to applying anti-scabies lotion. But this particular priest didn't seem to hear what I had said – he just continued to look out of the window of the car we were in. So I would repeat my request and say, 'Father, what about the soap?' But he would look back at me as if to say that the most important thing was that he had spotted this other development worker from the car and that he might meet him at the hotel swimming-pool one afternoon, or perhaps would invite him round for dinner that evening. I'm not saying that these people weren't doing good work – it's just that their priorities seemed to me to be all wrong.

Luckily, he could also vent this wrath in letters to Father Cunnane. In one such letter, one of many to find its way to Wales, Jack wrote:

I think your Irish priests and nuns are fantastic out here, but dear God the Bengali hierarchy is straight out of Hochhuth. And the Anglican is much on a par. Still, it's sensible to face up to what the Church actually is out here. Which is an organization which can turn virtually a blind eye, at least officially, to a political situation which verges on fascism. It does this to safeguard one million Christians here. Is it right? N O.

Nor was Preger the only Catholic to criticize the role of his own Church in relation to the Biharis. For in 1973, Father Gus, a Holy Ghost Father and a veteran of the famine in Biafra, told the Catholic Bishops of Bangladesh that, come the Day of Judgement, they would 'burn for their sins of omission', a sentiment with which Jack wholeheartedly agreed.

Within six years of his baptism in Ireland, Jack Declan Preger was surely as disenchanted with the Catholic Church as it is possible to be. But at least he was now able to place his views within a carefully considered political context. And there was more than the odd touch of dialectic in the conclusions he had reached:

I regard the Christian Church both in Dacca and Calcutta as bourgeois-orientated institutions far removed from both the teachings and example of Christ. These Churches, in their social work, provide, in my view, band-aid therapy which disguises, but does not heal, the wounds inflicted on destitutes etc. by the systematized exploitation of the Bangladesh and West Bengal economies. Their role is as reactionary in this respect as that of Lions and Rotary clubs. Nor do I support these Churches in their proselytizing, which is aimed, I believe, at strengthening their power-base, rather than the salvation of souls.

Jack's comments would distress the Irish priest, who continued to work with his congregation in Cardiganshire. But that did not deter him from regularly sending financial contributions to Jack's campaigns. Wherever Jack was, whatever he was doing, Father Cunnane and his parishioners were constantly to hand, raising funds and promptly dispatching them to the East in order to support his work, however radical it might be.

Jack may have found it grim in Bangladesh, especially during the early seventies. But lighter moments did occur, and they were usually attributable to the efforts of the volunteers themselves. Aware that it was important to switch off from the horror stories, which were seldom in short supply, the relief workers of Bangladesh would organize regular gatherings. These social occasions provided opportunities to share experiences, to swap notes, to drink, dance and sing. Irish ballads would be sung; English folk-songs too. What of Jack's contribution? It was certainly not a Catholic hymn. His party piece was a song drawn from the rich folk-lore of Yiddish, a language for which he retained a deep affection. It was a song to the accompaniment of a guitar and entitled '*Der Rebe Elimeylekh*', a Yiddish version of the English song, 'Old King Cole'.

Az der Rebe Elimeylekh
Iz gevorn zeyer freylekh
Is gevorn zeyer freylekh, Elimeylekh
Hot er oysgeton di tfiln
Un hot ongeton di briln
Un geshikt nokh di diflers di tsvey
Un di fidldike fidlers

Hobn fidldik gefidlt
Hobn fidldik gefidlt, hobn zey

Un az der Rebe Elimeylekh
Iz gevorn nokh mer freylekh
Iz gevorn nokh mer freylekh, Elimeylekh
Hot er opgemakht havdole
Mitn shames Reb Faftole
Un geshikt nokh di payklers di tsvey

Un di paykldike payklers
Hobn paykldik gepayklt
Hobn paykldik gepayklt, hobn zey

(When Rabbi Elimeylekh was merry, he took off his phylacteries, put on his glasses, and summoned his two fiddlers. When he grew merrier, he took off his robe, donned his cap and summoned his two cymbalists. And when Rabbi Elimeylekh became ecstatic, he recited his Sabbath prayer and summoned his two drummers.)

Of course there was not a single person within earshot, or indeed within the entire territory of the new State of Bangladesh, who understood a single word of it. Yet the song was always a favourite at such gatherings. The consensus among both volunteers and professional relief workers was that these unintelligible lyrics probably had something to do with the film *Fiddler on the Roof*, although no one was quite sure.

There was another story that enlivened the dinner table for some time. Since Jack was on call every night at the children's hospital, there was often a string of messages for him when he returned to his quarters. One communication was apparently attempting to explain that there was a telephone message for him on the reverse side of the paper. It was a delightful piece of Bengali English: 'Massage for Doctor Jack. Please turn to back side.'

If Jack had been 'dazzled by the great good he could do as a doctor' when he set out for Bangladesh, he soon realized that these laudable aspirations would have to be amended if he was to preserve his sanity. The plight of the Bihari refugees, the hopelessly inadequate medical facilities of Dacca, the lack of decent sanitation, housing and educational provision – they comprised a formidable agenda for just one medic. A Chinese proverb showed the way; an idealistic yet practical slogan that Jack adopted as his own: 'It is better to light a single candle somewhere in the world than to curse the darkness.' In fact Jack had done both. When he returned to England from Bangladesh in February 1974, there was no doubt at all that he had made one small part of the world a good deal lighter.

Four weeks later, no longer working with the destitutes of Dacca, Jack was himself confined to bed at his mother's home in Southport, suffering from shingles. It was a source of some alarm to the health authorities in Lancashire, since they were initially unable to rule out the possibility of smallpox, still rampant in Bangladesh.

On recovering, Jack returned to Ireland, where he took up a post as a locum registrar in a psychiatric hospital. Once again his world had undergone a radical transformation. Here was a job to which Leslie would no doubt have given fraternal approval. Material comforts, all but non-existent in Bangladesh, began to flow thick and fast. A respectable salary was earned; a rather nice Volkswagen Beetle acquired. Nor could the accommodation have been in a more spectacular setting: the gate-lodge of Castle Leslie in Co. Monaghan, just south of the border with Ulster. It would have been a seductive package to many doctors. But not for Jack Preger, as he explains:

> I was living in the most beautiful place imaginable – Dawson's Lodge, it was called – which was then on lease to the Irish playwright Wolf Mankowitz. And every day I used to ask myself, 'What the hell are you doing here?' I wasn't sure what to do next, and was doing these kind of fill-in jobs. I had everything that you could want materially, but not much more besides.

It was while sitting alone in the gate-lodge one day in the spring of 1974 that Jack had an experience that was to have the most profound impact on the rest of his life. The vacuum of which Jack had been complaining was about to be filled beyond his wildest expectations.

I didn't know it at the time, but in terms of the church calendar it was Pentecost. I suddenly experienced a sensation of great peacefulness, and received this message: 'I am the Paraclete.' It wasn't a voice, thank goodness, just a thought being put into my head. It was a really beautiful feeling of comfort and my whole mental state was completely changed for a few seconds.

In Christian theology the Paraclete, or Holy Spirit, is the third person of the Trinity. Numerous outpourings of the Spirit are mentioned in the Acts of the Apostles, in which healing, prophecy, the expulsion of demons and speaking in tongues are closely associated with the activity of the Spirit.

The crux of the matter, though, was that up until that time I had no idea what the word 'Paraclete' meant. I really had no idea at all – that's why I now feel that I was directed or taught what the Spirit means. If the message had been 'I am the Holy Spirit', well, I would have said, 'Yes, I know all that', and it wouldn't have meant anything special to me. I didn't bother to look up the word for a few days. But when I did so the dictionary referred me to the Gospel according to St John. Then I started to read everything I could about the Paraclete and I found that Christ had said, 'I will give you this Paraclete, this comforter, and with Him you will do greater miracles than I have done.' I then thought that this is Christ at Pentecost handing on the Holy Spirit and that this must surely be an indication not only of the existence of the Holy Spirit but of the role of Christ in transmitting the Holy Spirit. I do believe that just that one touch was the Spirit, and that once this has happened to you, you then have no choice but to do as the Spirit directs you.

For Jack, it was no hardship to do as instructed in this way. In fact the feeling associated with the Holy Spirit was exhilarating indeed, rekindling memories of years gone by:

It was such a beautiful feeling – the kind of sensation I had not experienced since childhood. It wasn't a manic feeling, like lights

112

flashing or Beethoven booming – it was just as if my mind had been caught hold of by something rather wonderful and cushioned from tensions of all kind. I remember one Monday morning when I was six years old. For some reason or other my mother had given me a really good scrubbing on the Sunday evening. My hair was washed and I had gone to bed straight away with fresh pyjamas. The following morning I was given some more clean clothes and as I was walking down the hill to school, the sun was out and I could see the Pennines. I felt so clean and happy to be alive. That was back in 1936. Well it was exactly the same feeling in 1974 when I had this Paraclete experience – that same feeling of total freshness.

On the word 'Paraclete' the dictionary gives additional guidance: 'one called to aid or support'. After several years of searching, striving, probing and questioning, Jack Preger had finally found a role. Now his mind was made up. It had been made up for him. He would return to Bangladesh, still desperate for both aid and support, where 'great miracles would be performed'. Jack's vision of the message of the Holy Spirit was not narrow and crabbed, nor confined within the bounds of academic theological debate. Here was a practical proposition, inextricably bound up with the whole issue of human rights. Nor was he convinced that Christians somehow had exclusive access to the message of the Spirit. For Preger, the Paraclete was above all a rallying call to action: to get the work done, for the sake of God.

Jack made contact with the Paraclete in 1974. He also made renewed contact with Cathy that same year. Having been abandoned by her husband, with whom she had had three children, Cathy was more than pleased that Jack had got in touch. But whereas Maritta could plead ignorance of Jack's commitment to the Third World when their romance had first blossomed, Cathy could not. For by now Jack had not only spent two years working in Bangladesh, but had also made it abundantly clear that he had every intention of returning there as soon as possible. With the power of the Paraclete propelling him, there could surely now be no misunderstanding as to the future direction of his life; it was to alleviate the plight of the poor. This might well have been an extremely precarious basis on which to develop an intimate relationship, especially for a woman who now sought security and stability for herself and her children. But Cathy wanted Jack; she had always wanted Jack. And, for the moment at least, Jack wanted Cathy.

Free of his commitments in Ireland, Jack returned to Bangladesh in 1975 and accepted a job as a medical officer at the dispensary in Dacca of a Dutch organization known as Terre des Hommes. Here was an international agency whose aims and objectives were honourable indeed. Its charter spelled out the aims and objectives of the charity: Terre des Hommes was 'dedicated to relief, development, rehabilitation and the adoption of children'. And its members appeared to be as good as their word. For it was with their financial assistance that Jack managed to set up a clinic for destitutes at Kamlapur railway station in Dacca. But this was not the only work in which the doctor became involved. Through a contact of Father Cunnane's, Jack helped to organize a camp for destitute children with funds received from a British registered trust, the International Boys' Town.

As if there were not enough projects to occupy his time, Jack launched himself into the building of a ninety-bed clinic, the Khan Sahib Azizul Islam Memorial Clinic, of which he was appointed director. He had persuaded a local property owner, a Muslim, to allow the roof of his warehouse in South Kamlapur to be converted into a clinic for the poor of Dacca. The Muslim sought not a penny in rent, in one of those kindly acts referred to by Mother Teresa as 'something beautiful for God'. The funding of this clinic was international, the House of Charity, a Minneapolis-based American relief organization, providing money for the building work, while the clinic's equipment was purchased by a Canadian bankers' trust.

Delighted with the doctor's work, the Government of Bangladesh promised to lease out land where Preger could resettle families of Bihari refugees, whose unfortunate plight had changed little and was never far from his mind. Thriving on the numerous

Jack's parents, Bertha and Harold Preger, who owned a thriving grocery business in Manchester.

The Pregers' three children. Left to right: Leslie, Anita and Jack.

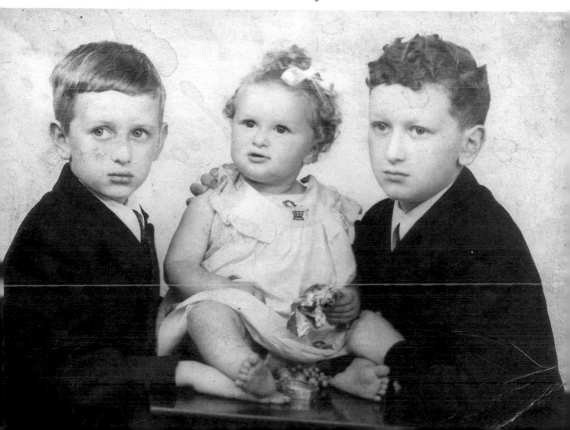

Punting at Oxford. Jack read PPE at St Edmund Hall and was regarded as part of the 'lunatic fringe'.

Gernos Farm, in Wales, where Jack and Maritta's son, Alun (visible), was born.

Jack (front row, right) at the Royal College of Surgeons in Dublin, 1971.

Maritta and Alun in London after their separation from Jack.

Cathy and Jack on their wedding day in 1977. Jack, accompanied by his new wife, returned to Bangladesh almost immediately after the ceremony.

One of Calcutta's familiar invalid tricycles. This one was inscribed with the Gaelic *Pog Mo Thoin* by Satty, the Irish volunteer who donated it to the clinic.

Dr Jack Preger.

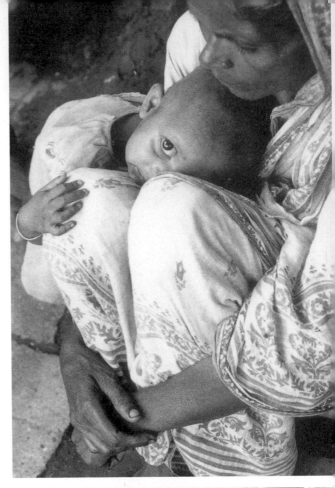

At the street clinic in
Middleton Row up to 400
patients are seen each day.

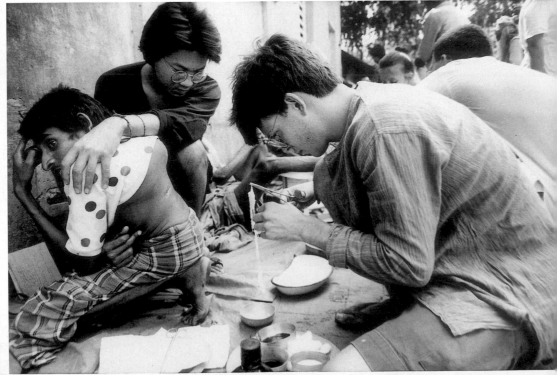

Calcutta's destitutes flock to the narrow strip of pavement where Dr Jack holds his clinic; examinations are free.

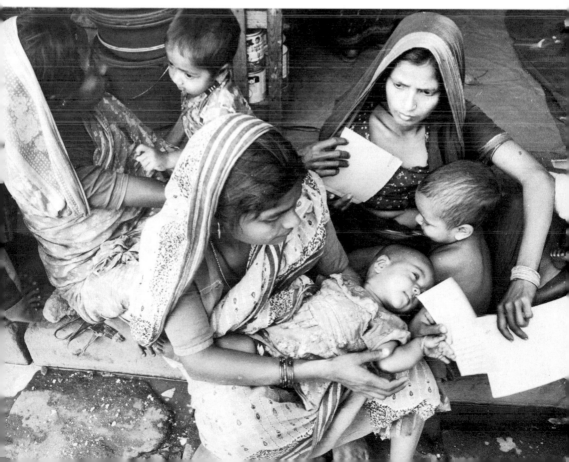

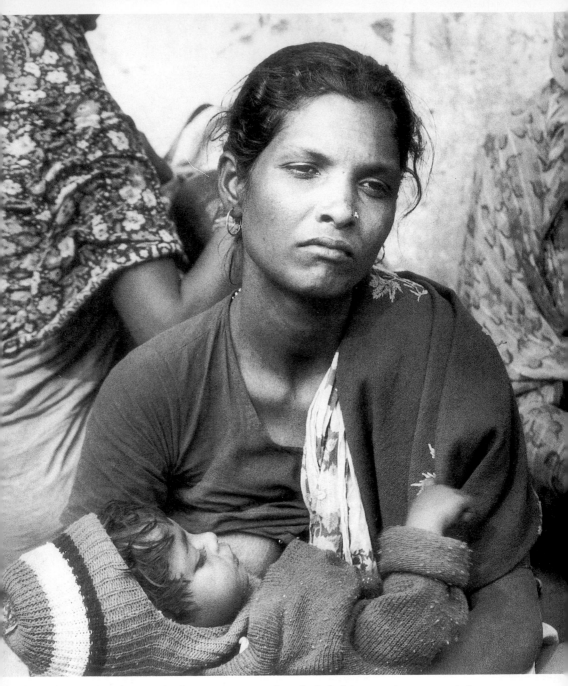

Mothers queue for hours to ensure that their babies are given essential vaccinations.

challenges before him, Jack secured additional foreign funding, which led to the purchase of a farm at Eniatpur, some thirty kilometres from Dacca, on which twenty refugee families were duly settled. It was no match for the majestic setting of Gernos, but one thing was certain: Jack was considerably more fulfilled working with the vagrants of Bangladesh than he ever was in rural Wales. This was the sort of relief work that combined Jack's skills as a medical practitioner with his many years of experience as a farmer familiar with the principles of economics. In fact a considerable part of what Asa Briggs had taught Preger at Oxford proved extremely useful to him in Bangladesh. Thrilled with the progress and confident that at last he had found his niche, Jack wrote to Father Cunnane about the good work in hand. More candles had been lit to dispel a little of the darkness:

> The Boys' Town continues to spread and we have thirty-five boys now on a smallholding some eleven miles from Dacca which is leased from the Archbishop of Dacca. There are twenty-five other boys in a camp we are building not far from the Archbishop's land, which is meant primarily for cleared slum-dwellers from Dacca. Another group of boys remain in Kamlapur and we've started a spinning and weaving programme for them, as well as a carpentry course. The future of the slum-dwellers' camp is very uncertain but at least for now they have somewhere to stay.

Jack was doing wonders for the people of Bangladesh. But not for his ageing and ailing mother, who remained in Southport. Often she did not hear from her son for several months. Aware that Jack had been involved in work that put him at risk, especially since he had aligned himself with the Bihari refugees, Bertha asked her daughter Anita to make contact with the British High Commission in Dacca. If something dreadful had happened to her son, it was imperative that she be kept informed. The High Commission responded by sending its First Secretary and two junior officials to track down the doctor. Jack had been out of Dacca for some time, busy running the newly acquired land. The First Secretary delivered his message with the full weight of Her Majesty's Government behind him: 'Jack, you haven't rung your mother.'

It was during the spring of 1977 that Preger stumbled on a business that, for any normal person, let alone a religious man, must surely have epitomized evil. For he encountered evidence of a black-market traffic in children abducted from their parents. Moreover, there appeared to be evidence of a kidnapping ring willing to supply children not only for illegal adoption but also for prostitution, pornography, mutilation and murder. But were these allegations of a vague and general nature, or did they point to particular organizations and individuals? In fact parents were complaining that it was Preger's own employers, Terre des Hommes, that had tricked them into handing over their children under false pretences. At first Jack refused to be drawn into the controversy. Here were allegations that were surely too far-fetched and fanciful to be true.

> I was at the Terre des Hommes clinic in Dacca when a senior clinic staff member told me about this racket. Then, when I started to work in my own clinic, mothers who knew that I used to work with Terre des Hommes came to me and complained that they had lost their children through tricks of various kinds. I ignored their protests to begin with, because I knew this one might really mean trouble. But then a French nurse, Elizabeth Seytel, with whom I had been working for some time, turned to me and said, 'Well, aren't you going to do anything at all about it then?' Anyway, I got involved.

It was an involvement that would later lead to Preger's deportation from Bangladesh. In taking up this latest challenge was he not stepping well outside his role as a purely medical man? Surely matters of such gravity were best dealt with by the police? But even if such reasoning was correct, it was advice that failed to convince Jack. If a doctor needs to be a policeman, then a policeman he should be:

> I just can't see this as stepping outside of the world of medicine, because you are supposed to be working as a medical officer.

Well, with these poor people, losing their children is one of the biggest afflictions that could possibly happen to them. My view was that if there was something I could do, then I should do it.

And he did, beginning by taking affidavits from parents in a relief camp at Dattapara, from which a hundred children had mysteriously been removed. In fact Jack's investigations soon bore fruit. Before long the doctor-detective was confident that he had successfully identified the man behind the racket. His name was Moslem Ali Khan. Jack knew Khan rather well, for the simple reason that Khan happened to be the Director of Terre des Hommes, his former boss. Khan also ran a Dutch adoption agency known as the Inter-Country Child Welfare Organisation. It soon became apparent that Khan's priority was not so much the welfare of the child as the welfare of his own pocket.

Khan's partners were also deeply involved in the abduction, sale and disposal of Bangladesh's babies. One was a New Zealander by the name of Alan Cheyne, head of the Underprivileged Children's Education Programme; another, Dr Mizanur Rahman Shelley, head of the Bangladesh Directorate of Social Welfare, the department responsible for processing the papers authorizing legal adoptions in that country.

Jack was in no doubt: Khan, Cheyne and Shelley were callous criminals whose cynical activities had to be exposed. This powerful trio, in Jack's opinion, were perfectly placed to dispose of the missing children. Allegedly using the legitimate programmes they ran as a front, Khan and Cheyne were able to round up the victims, while Dr Shelley, in charge of issuing visas, handled the paperwork needed to ship them out of the country. Having obtained the names of thirty-five children who had fallen into their hands, Jack learned that Khan and Cheyne had bought them airline tickets for Amsterdam. He presented his evidence to the Dutch authorities, who could account for only six of the thirty-five children. When the doctor then asked to examine the KLM flight manifests, the airline refused, claiming that it was not convinced that the children had been fraudulently obtained, even though several were over the legal age for adoption in the Netherlands.

With Jack's encouragement and financial backing, many of the parents took their cases to lawyers in Dacca. Their affidavits make grim reading, as is illustrated by the case of Mr Matiur Rahman, just one among many. The text is reproduced here as in the original document:

BEFORE MY MOLLAH. M HAQUE, NOTARY PUBLIC, BANGLADESH, DHAKA.

I, Mr. Matiur Rahman S/O L. Fazlul Karim Howladar aged about 35 years presently residing at Block No. 6, Dattapara Camp, Tongi, Dacca, Bangladesh by religion a muslim do hereby solemnly affirm and state as under:–

1. That (1) Mr Moslem Ali Khan S/O Torab Ali Khan and (2) Mr Humayun Kabir S/O Sundar Ali of Terre Des Hommes Netherland in 1977 have taken from me my minor daughters named Nilu – 9 years, Laily – 7 years and Momtaz – 9 months at that time saying that they would take the children to Dhanmondi Baby Home for their maintenance and education.

2. That I was a Rickshaw Driver in 1977 and quite unable to feed and maintain the expenses of the children, so I gave them for their better education.

3. That the above named gentlemen gave me hope that I would be entitled to see the children once in week.

4. That after some time I went to Dhanmondi Terre des Hommes office but I was not allowed to see the children.

5. That till now I have not heard any news of the children and I suspect that the children have been sold to foreign countries.

6. That I was told the children shall remain in Dacca as my own children.

7. That I was not given any compensation.

8. That Mr Hossain and Mr Humayun of Terre des Hommes office warned me and show me pistol and asked me to tell to the Director of social welfare (when Dr M. Rahman came to Tongi) that I did give the children according to my own wish.

9. That they would kill me they said by pistol if I would not say in their favour in the enquiry.

10. That now I want justice and punishment of the above persons.

11. That I want back my children.

12. That I immediately like to know the whereabouts of my daughters and communication with them.

13. That I have been cheated by Mr Moslem Ali Khan, Director, Terre des Hommes (Netherland).

14. That I do hereby authorize M/S H and H Company, Barristers at Law, 56/57 Motijheel C/A Dacca to look into my case and arrange to get back my children on humanitarian ground.

The Statement made above are true to the best of my knowledge and belief.

It was for Nilu, Laily and Momtaz – and all of the other missing children – that Preger embarked on a campaign to expose these alleged racketeers. The doctor's philosophy was hardly complex: 'That these children are missing,' he wrote to Father Cunnane, 'is sufficient reason that they be found.' Some victims had simply been snatched from the streets. Others, as in the case cited above, were taken from their parents with the promise that they would be sent to a boarding-school. Many illiterate, poverty-stricken parents, in a country where the average daily wage remains well under one pound sterling, were deceived into giving up their offspring in the belief that they would be fed, housed and educated by Terre des Hommes. Assured that they could visit their children at any time, the parents discovered when they attempted to do so that not only did the schools not exist, but that their children had vanished without trace. And then the final trick in this complex web of deceit: parents were informed that the blank papers on which they had made their thumbprints were forms by which they had formally relinquished their sons and daughters for adoption.

While it was clear to Jack that he was beginning to tread on toes, it did not cross his mind to remove the pressure he was applying. However, Khan was perfectly capable of giving as good as he got, promising Jack that it would not be long before he would have his revenge. The kindest fate awaiting those children spirited away from Bangladesh was the prospect of illegal adoption overseas by parents prepared to pay a thousand pounds or more. About the rest of the kidnap victims, few can speak with certainty. But it is no secret in Dacca that children are sold to professional beggars' syndicates and mutilated to increase their earning potential, as Jack can testify:

I used to examine a number of these beggars. They would be put out each morning by the syndicate and collected, with their earnings, in the evening. Some would have severe malformations of the limbs which were not the result of congenital problems, but had been acquired by binding up the limbs for long periods. I also found in some cases that their 'injuries' were surprisingly similar. It was as if somebody had learned how to do a certain amputation and just went on doing it, as if on an assembly line.

For those children who escaped disfigurement, there was the prospect of being sold into a brothel or introduced into other kinds of sexual commerce. A UN report on the international traffic in children explains:

Begging doesn't really bring in big money. Pornography does. The biggest income comes from the very young children, down to the ages of two and three years old. They are filmed and photographed in acts of paedophilia and even with animals. You can buy these cassettes at kiosks all over the world and project them at home. And there are the so-called 'snuff' films now on the market in which teenage girls are actually put to death.

Preger was not seeking to suggest that the missing children of Dattapara were featuring in pornographic films, although one set of parents were convinced that they could recognize their seven-year-old daughter in an illegal Danish pornographic magazine that was brought to their attention. The truth was that no one really knew what had become of their children. For the unfortunate parents it was a torture many times worse than mourning the death of a child, as Jack explains:

When a child dies at least the mother knows that a grave exists or the ashes went this way or that. But as for the kidnapping – well, it's a living death. I've been with mothers going around Dacca looking for their children and it's a pitiful sight to watch. On occasions like this I have prayed to the Virgin Mary – that this is beyond anything that any mother should ever have to suffer.

In the middle of this growing scandal in which accusations were being bandied about in every direction, Jack decided that he should marry Cathy. While attending medical school in Dublin he had been reluctant to give Cathy the commitment she sought. Now, ten years later, and after a few times together during his twice-yearly visits to England, he was apparently willing to do so. But the truth of the matter was that the passage of a decade had brought about little or no change in Jack's enthusiasm for marriage:

I had known Cathy for many years, and loved her for many years too. But she talked me into marrying her at the last minute. There was great reluctance on my part and I did argue against it. In fact I had so many doubts that before leaving Bangladesh for England, I went to see a priest and spoke to him about how I was uncertain if things would work out for us. But I did think that we might be able to get things together in Bangladesh. It was a gamble, I know, but everything is a gamble really.

Jack reluctantly placed his bet, and a date for the wedding was agreed. Since Cathy had still to obtain her annulment, the wedding took place at Canterbury Registry Office in October 1977. Whereas no Pregers had been present at the Chelsea Registry Office when, twenty years earlier, Jack and Maritta had wed, this time members of Jack's family attended the ceremony. Leslie could not come, but his sister Anita did, together with her husband and two daughters. And what of Bertha's attitude? Maritta had paid a high price for having been brought up in the Church of England. Bertha's first grandchild, Alun, had done likewise and been deprived of all contact with his grandmother. In fact during all his seventeen years, they had spoken together only once, and that by telephone. Was there, then, any compelling reason why Bertha should suddenly warm to Cathy, a divorced Roman Catholic and mother of three children? Apparently there was. Now well into her mid-seventies, Bertha appeared to have changed. For when Anita asked her why she had rejected Maritta and the boy, but had been prepared to accept Cathy and her three children, the old lady replied pragmatically, 'Because I do not want to lose my son.'

If Bertha was ready to make an effort, so too was Cathy. The night before the wedding, the bride-to-be went to some trouble to find caterers who would be able to provide a meal capable of meeting the strict dietary requirements of the *kashrut*. It was a gesture very much appreciated by Bertha. But when the reception got under way, she apparently concluded that the best way to cope with the considerable stress of the occasion was to resort to drink.

While these rather strained celebrations were taking place, a number of telegrams had arrived from Bangladesh. Jack's contacts there were anxious to warn him that the government was beginning to crack down on his various activities. Moslem Ali Khan had been fighting back. The storm over the illegal traffic in children was about to break. If any of the wedding guests thought that this might deter the newly-wed doctor from returning to that country, they would have been mistaken. As for Cathy, despite being asked to fly with Jack to Bangladesh at the first available opportunity, she remained confident that the marriage would flourish. She recalls:

We never lived together in England, because we all went out to Bangladesh together. He had what appeared to be a fairly stable situation out there at that time, running the clinic for street destitutes. And I very much believed in his work. I took my three children out to Dacca with me and they enrolled at one of the local schools. It was all a bit terrifying at first, and for a while I didn't want to go out at all. I was mainly involved with looking after my children. Maybe I should have seen the writing on the wall, because when I arrived in Bangladesh there were some women running an organization called Families for Children. Well, when they saw me they just laughed and said, 'Fancy him getting married' – they knew that he just wasn't the marrying sort. And there was something else which, with hindsight, perhaps I should have read more accurately. Because I remember being absolutely amazed when, shortly after we had arrived in Bangladesh, Jack said that he might start commuting to Calcutta in order to help the destitutes there. I just said to myself, 'Well, how much of him am I going to see?'

The government of Bangladesh was not at all pleased to have Jack Preger back in their country. Having taken his file on the missing children to the authorities in Dacca, Jack himself was now the subject of investigation. Khan, Cheyne and Shelley, alleged by Jack to be behind the scandal, had been hard at work during his absence abroad, prodding the police into all kinds of activities. A comprehensive search had been conducted at the British Council library in Dacca to check if the doctor's name was on the list of British medical practitioners. And when the authorities learned of Jack's Jewish ancestry, it was not long before reports of his being a 'Zionist spy' began to circulate in the city. And if he was not a bogus doctor, an Israeli secret agent or a member of the CIA, there was always the last recourse of linking him with missionary activities of various kinds.

While Jack steadfastedly refused to be either silenced or intimidated, the prospect of deportation proceedings drew ever closer. He retained a Bangladeshi lawyer, Nazmul Huda, who, as secretary-general of the Bangladesh Society for the Enforcement of Human Rights, was well placed to protect Jack's interests. Jack managed to persuade Huda, at that time also acting as legal counsel for the American Embassy in Dacca, to interview the parents in Dattapara himself. What Jack did not know was that Huda also had Alan Cheyne as a client, one of the three against whom he had made allegations. Huda made a half-hearted attempt to take affidavits at Dattapara, but soon caved in to political pressure. As the lawyer later revealed:

I was advised by the Home Minister not to fight the case. So this was coming from the horse's mouth. Jack Preger had certain permits to carry out his work in Bangladesh without meddling in any affairs. But he got involved in so many problems like this that people found him an interference with the government. In my opinion, Jack Preger was a very sincere person who was trying to unfold certain wrongs that had been committed by certain powerful government officials in collaboration with some private agencies like Terre des Hommes and Moslem Ali Khan. He was really out to see that justice was done. The problem was that he was a foreigner and as such could be deported.

There was one speedy and effective way to avoid deportation. Jack could choose to do something that had become quite unfamiliar: hold his tongue. In fact he did the opposite. In shouting his story from the rooftops of Dacca, he was well aware that it would not be long before he would find himself on a flight out of Bangladesh. It was fortunate for Khan and his associates that the notion of compromise was quite alien to Jack:

I told the government what was going on. I told all kinds of people the details. Then the authorities gave me an option of paying 15,000 *taka*, about £500, for which they would issue me with a visa renewal. If I would have paid this simple £500 bribe, then I dare say Cathy and I and the children would all still be there. But to do so just stuck in my throat. That these criminals were going to take £500 of people's donations. Our main donor, the Catholic mission, advised me to cough up. But the idea of putting this money, their money, into the hands of these people, these murderers – it was just not on.

With deportation now imminent, Jack went to the Ministry of Health to plead not for himself but his patients. In a meeting with a Joint Secretary, one of the Ministry's top officials, he pointed out that deportation would mean that many of the patients in his ninety-bed clinic would die. The senior civil servant turned to Preger. His response was hardly laden with compassion:

'Well, let them die.'

And they did. Police came to arrest Jack at the clinic in February 1979. He had been persuaded by the French nurse, Elizabeth Seytel, not to resist arrest, in the hope that the government might allow foreign nurses to continue to work at the clinic. It was an error of judgement on her part, for not long after Jack's arrest the patients were unceremoniously dumped on the pavement outside. A local doctor who used to work at the clinic later informed Jack that he had seen one patient die in front of the clinic that very day. Other deaths followed soon after.

It was the Bangladeshi Special Branch, responsible for dealing with enemy aliens, who came to oversee the deportation of the doctor. He was driven back to his flat to gather some belongings. Cathy was there with her three children. It was a deportation with a distinctly civilized air, Cathy serving tea to the men with orders to expel her husband from Bangladesh. After collecting his passport, Jack tucked his spectacles into his shirt pocket and was driven to the airport, where he was made to board a plane for Singapore.

Two years earlier Moslem Ali Khan had vowed that he would one day exact his revenge. Unlike his pledges to the parents of the missing children, this time he had kept his word.

8
Quit India

as from 8 Park Avenue
Southport
Merseyside

Easter Monday 1979

Dear Father,
A Happy Easter to you and all in Cardigan.

I have to convey some bad news — that I was deported from
Dacca after the Government refused visa renewals; and Cathy
and the children were also forced to leave after I had gone. We are
at the moment with Cathy's parents in Hunstanton, Norfolk, but
I spend some time with my mother in Southport. We were
involved in a long-standing row with the Bangladesh Directorate
of Social Welfare over allegations about an adoption racket they
were running. And over conditions in their Vagrants' Homes. In
the end the Social Welfare took over our programme, although I
have tried to transfer our assets to other organizations in
Bangladesh.

An enquiry is now starting in Europe about the adoption
business and there is some hope of Bangladeshis in Britain
organizing a petition to get me a new visa. However, I have no
real hope that the Bangladesh Government will change its mind
quickly.

It was another of Jack's messages to the priest. But whereas any other person in Jack's position would surely have deemed Third World work an experience not to be repeated, Jack's aspirations had been revised rather than abandoned. The new plan was to go to Calcutta to seek a job there instead.

However, before setting out in June for the East, Jack embarked on an energetic press campaign to highlight the scandal of the adoptions. The newspapers were in no doubt: the doctor's story was good copy. Charles Nevin, a journalist working for the *Daily Telegraph*, wrote a particularly hard-hitting article, which was given some prominence by his editor. As the headline 'I FOUND ADOPTION RACKET', CLAIMS DEPORTED DOCTOR reverberated around the world, questions began to be asked. The Anti-Slavery Society backed Jack's case. The London-based Minority Rights Group did likewise. Back in England, Preger vigorously lobbied MPs, some of whom tabled a series of parliamentary questions in the House of Commons.

Invited to investigate the affair in Holland, where Terre des Hommes had its headquarters, Jack found that whereas his initial detective work in Dacca had been relatively easy, he was now quite unable to make any progress with the case. Wherever he went, whoever he contacted, the answer was invariably the same: no one knew anything. Nor could any official from any department in any country explain how it was that a number of children had come to be separated from their parents, or indeed what had become of them. A picket launched outside the Bangladeshi High Commission in London proved equally fruitless. The approach of the Bangladeshi government was consistent if nothing else: it was a matter of much regret, officials would inform the doctor, but they were entirely unaware of any irregularities, alleged or otherwise, relating to the adoption of children in their country.

A television appearance by Jack on a current affairs programme resulted in one lead, though entirely unrelated to the adoption issue. The programme, produced by Manchester-based Granada Television, told how local boy Preger had come to embrace the cause of the Biharis. A Mrs Greenhauch happened to be watching TV in her bedroom when she became convinced that she had spotted a familiar face.

'Hey, Gertie, its our Jackie on television!', she shouted down the stairs to her daughter.

Forty years had elapsed since young Jackie had been evacuated to the Greenhauchs' home in Mellor, yet the old lady recognized him at once. Contact was renewed, telephone numbers exchanged. For the Bangladeshis, by contrast, the wave of unfavourable publicity generated by the campaigning doctor had an entirely predictable effect. Retreating into its shell, the High Commission refused to respond to Jack and the Press alike.

The idea of setting out for Calcutta had not suddenly appeared out of thin air. In the spring of 1978 Jack had written to Father Cunnane, informing him, with characteristic perversity, that he was tempted to seek work in India's former capital.

'It may well happen that I end up by working in Calcutta,' the doctor had confided to his friend, 'because that is where things are still bad indeed.'

In fact they were extremely bad, the city as ever demonstrating its ability to provoke the very strongest of reactions. Writing in 1863, the British historian Sir George Trevelyan had challenged his readers to 'find, if you can, a more uninviting spot than Calcutta . . . it unites every condition of a perfectly unhealthy situation . . . The place is so bad by nature that human efforts could do little to make it worse; but that little has been done faithfully and assiduously.'

And still more had been done by 12 August 1979, the day on which Jack packed his bags and set out for Calcutta, the teeming capital of West Bengal, Kipling's 'City of Dreadful Night'. Immediately on arrival he applied for official permission to remain in Calcutta and run a clinic. Aware that his papers had to be in order, Jack registered with both the police and the Ministry of Relief and Social Welfare, whose officials were, initially at least, both helpful and encouraging. While working part-time with Mother Teresa's Brothers of Charity as a lay volunteer, Jack managed to initiate a couple of small feeding programmes in the Strand Road and Jagannath Ghat areas of the city. And that was in addition to opening a makeshift clinic for destitutes under the flyover near

Calcutta's famous Howrah Bridge, whose colossal steel mesh is some four feet longer by day than by night.

The following spring Preger shifted his clinic to St Thomas's Church in Middleton Row, where the vicar had offered him a room. It was a relief to get off the streets, as Jack recalls:

I was living in the YWCA international guest house in Middleton Row, so when the priest of St Thomas's offered me the gate-lodge of his presbytery garden for the stocking of medicines and patients' records, it was extremely convenient. What happened, though, was that the destitutes in and around the Middleton Row area soon found out that this was my new base and would drop in for medical attention or some food. Well, the priests didn't like that at all. They told me that it was all right as a storeroom, but not as a clinic. Just about the same time as this was happening, the Calcutta Municipal Development Authority decided that the area under the flyover of Howrah Bridge, where I was working, should be developed. They put up high railings where I used to run my programme and simply displaced the hundreds of destitutes who used to squat there. In the end I told all my out-patients that it was impossible to see them in the old locations, scattered around the city – in any case they were not there any more – and that they should come up to Middleton Row instead.

From Jack's perspective it was the most logical thing to do. This logic, however, was not appreciated by the parish priest of St Thomas's. As the poor and needy of Calcutta began to clutter the church, the priest decided that Preger would have to go, and sooner rather than later. The doctor was informed that since it was the intention of the church to have gas meters installed in the gate-lodge, patients milling in and around the area posed an unacceptable risk. It was hardly a sophisticated ploy, but it served its purpose. Although not a single gas meter was ever installed, Jack had received the cleric's message and decided to move on.

But Jack did not go very far; only a few yards in fact. To the fury of the parish priest, he started a makeshift clinic on the narrow pavement directly outside the church. He has been there ever since, to the irritation of church and corporation alike. Jack had been working in India for less than a year before he had once again engaged in battle with the authorities. It was not so much that he enjoyed a fight; rather that remaining silent about injustice was a stance that was ever more difficult to sustain. And in Calcutta, as in Bangladesh, there was never any shortage of injustice.

Of course beating up prisoners is by no means unique to Calcutta. But such systematic beating by the West Bengali police was an abuse of human rights that the doctor was able to observe at close quarter. However, it was some time before Jack felt able to reflect on this brutality with a mixture of irony and anger:

Working with the destitutes of Calcutta used to bring me into contact with the police quite a lot. I would on occasion use their telephone to get an ambulance. They were usually most courteous with me, and would even stop beating up the prisoners when I walked in. I remember going in one day to ask permission to use their phone, only to be told that the inspectors were out in the back. I walked into this room at the back of the police station where there were these two giant policeman each holding a great length of rope and two chaps cowering on the floor just dressed in their *lunghis*, stripped to the waist and having the guts beaten out of them. I walked in and gave a sort of diplomatic cough.

'I wonder if I could possibly use your phone to call for an ambulance?' I said.

The policemen looked at me like embarrassed giants, each of them hiding the rope behind his back. After a short pause they replied, 'Yes, please, do go ahead' – and then breathed an almighty sigh of relief as I left and they resumed their ferocious beating of the prisoners.

Jack soon became preoccupied with the plight of prisoners. Perhaps it was as well, because within the year he was to become one himself. Was there any evidence, though, of a similar anxiety to protect the rights of his own wife? Indeed, what had become of Cathy? True, Jack had explained in his letter to Father Cunnane that before he had set out for Calcutta, Cathy had been living in Norfolk while he was with his mother in Southport. This was the truth; but not the whole truth. Jack's simple statement concerning their respective whereabouts served to camouflage a serious rift that had cast a shadow over their marriage, still short of its third anniversary. As Cathy explains:

When we got deported from Bangladesh my parents offered us accommodation at their home in Norfolk, and I was surprised that Jack accepted because I knew it wouldn't be a good thing. Of course Jack was determined to get back to Bangladesh, and when that didn't work out he went back to Calcutta. I was prepared to go with him, but by that time he had had a huge rumpus with my parents. They really wanted him to settle down, and my mother really tried a bit too hard, as mothers will. So Jack went back to his own mother, and we hardly saw each other. It was all very traumatic. Despite all this I was still prepared to go out to Calcutta with the three children, because there was a sister school there to the one the children had attended in Dacca. I was working as an auxiliary nurse in Norwich, and doing my best to support the children when, unexpectedly, Jack said that his mother would have me to stay in Southport prior to his departure for Calcutta. So we all went up there for a few days. I was upset because there had been so little communication between us. But we did sleep together then. I was due to go out there at Christmas, although I must admit I was apprehensive. Whenever I asked Jack when we would be coming out to Calcutta he would say, 'Oh, I don't know if I could find anywhere for you to live out there.' In the end I hung on and hung on and hung on. I don't know why – probably because I had had a broken marriage before.

As rapidly as Jack was walking away from the ties of matrimony, so the impersonal wheels of the Indian legal system were catching up with him. In June 1980 the Security Control of the Calcutta police informed the doctor that he was obliged henceforth to be registered as a medical practitioner and missionary worker should he continue to practise in Calcutta. When he protested that he was not connected with any missionary or religious organization (although he did receive funds from the American Catholic Mission) the authorities appeared to accept his explanation and issued him a residential permit valid for three months. A Security Control official, Kumar Gaurav Bhattacharya, assured Jack that registration was nothing more than a formality.

The authorities were as good as their word. Jack's work was allowed to continue, but only for the duration of the residential permit. Once those three months had elapsed, it was time to leave India. Dismayed at receiving his first order to quit in September 1980, Preger rushed to the West Bengal secretariat to find out why he was being deported.

It was the beginning of a scenario that might have inspired Kafka. At the secretariat Jack was told that it was the Government of India that wanted to throw him out. When he travelled to New Delhi, he was informed that the Government of India had no objection to his staying. No, he was given to understand, it was the West Bengal government that was determined to see him go. Jack eventually cut through this vicious circle of bureaucracy thanks to the intervention of the New Delhi Ministry of Home Affairs, who cabled the government of West Bengal:

> Reference to our wireless message number 25017/11/90-FI dated 5 November regarding Jack Preger, a British National, further representation against quit India order received. Case being reconsidered. In the meantime he may be permitted to remain in the country pending final decision. Detailed letter follows.

Why such hostility from the government of West Bengal? Because since India gained independence in 1947 foreign mission workers have often been perceived as subversives promoting Christian ideals that could pose a threat to the traditional caste system. Certainly the Gospel according to St Matthew describes the basis of Christian missionary activity very clearly:

And Jesus came and spake unto them saying: All power is given unto me in heaven and in earth. Go, ye, therefore, and teach all nations, baptizing them in the name of the Father, and of the Son, and of the Holy Ghost: teaching them to observe all things whatsoever I have commanded you; and, lo, I am with you always, even unto the end of the world. Amen.

Christian missionaries have had a long relationship with India; they were part of the imperial forces' assault on the subcontinent. The preaching of Christianity and the salvaging of 'heathens' were key components of missionary activity for at least two centuries. One legacy of this is that being charitable in Calcutta is anything but an easy business, as Preger was discovering to his cost. Moreover, many of the city's residents distrust foreigners and several reputable aid agencies, Save the Children among them, have been barred. An atmosphere of suspicion prevails, so that foreign charity money must be accounted for to the last rupee and organizations that take it must be audited every six months.

The western concept of charity is so alien to the Hindu that many Indians simply do not believe that people like Dr Jack, as they know him, can be willing to devote their lives to caring for strangers. They feel that somewhere there must be a catch. To the Hindu, suffering is part of the unending cycle of life: pain today, but pleasure, hopefully, in the next incarnation. India and the concept of equity have never gone hand in hand. To this day much of Calcutta's industrial wealth rests in the hands of a small community of Marwari businessmen, originally from Rajasthan. It was only a few years ago during the drought in that region that the Marwaris collected money to send home; not for the hungry children but for the dying cows.

As for his precise legal status, Jack concedes that:

I did sign that declaration saying that I was a missionary worker, but only in the sense that I had accepted funds from that American missionary organization. Certainly there were never any religious strings attached to this funding – just so long as it went to the poor – and I've never carried out any conversion work of any kind. I signed that form against my better judgement: it was just a trick to get rid of me.

Missionary or no, there was another, more pragmatic, reason for wanting to evict Preger and his ilk: the fact that uncontrolled charity work inevitably attracts even more refugees to the great cities of India, already bursting with shanty towns. But what is most inconvenient for the governments of India, regional and national, is that the Pregers of this world persist in exposing the total inadequacy of existing health care provision for the poor. Despite its embarrassment the Indian establishment has not been shy about hitting back. According to Prasanta Sur, the Minister for Health for West Bengal, the issue is quite clear-cut:

'There is no problem in Calcutta and no need for Dr Preger to stay.'

It is a view with which Dr N. K. Mukarjee, the Superintendent of Calcutta's National Medical College Hospital, heartily concurs:

'We provide all the facilities and there is quite simply no need for foreigners to be involved.'

It came as no surprise to Jack when, in June 1981, he received a second order to quit from the Home Department of the Government of West Bengal. But since the order did not specifically state that he could not return to the country, Jack went to Kathmandu for five days, from where he re-entered India through Siliguri in north Bengal. Although officials at the Darjeeling border post refused to stamp his passport, they allowed the itinerant doctor to pass through. This time it did not take the authorities quite so long to catch up with their man. On 24 July 1981 Jack received a third, unequivocal order to quit:

No: 670 – PP(A) s-31/80:
In exercise of the power conferred by clause (c) of sub-section (2) of section 3 of the Foreigners Act, 1946 (XXXI of 1946), read with Government of India, Ministry of Home Affairs, Notification No. 4/3/56-(I) F. I. dated the 19th April 1958, the Governor is pleased hereby to order that
Shri: Jack Preger – Jacob Preger

a foreigner of British nationality, shall not remain in India after
the expiry of twenty-four hours from the time of service of this
order on him.
By order of the Governor

It might well have been an order of the Governor, but it was one
with which a number of international airlines were unable to assist.
The British High Commission intervened and succeeded in getting
the deadline extended to seventy-two hours, but the earliest departure Jack was able to arrange was for two days after that. Finally,
and reluctantly, Jack purchased a one-way ticket to England. It
seemed that his game of cat and mouse with the West Bengali
authorities was over. In the event it was quite impossible for the
doctor to catch even the later flight. The reason was that the
recipient of quit order number 670 found himself on the wrong side
of the walls of Alipore Special Jail at the time of its departure. From
Jack's point of view, though, he was on the right side:

> I was very interested to go into prison to see what it was like. I
> had heard so many stories of what was going on inside Indian
> prisons that I wanted to see for myself. It was my wish to remain
> in custody in order to expose the prison conditions in more detail
> afterwards.

As if Jack did not already have enough on his plate, he devoted a
good deal of his energies to finding out as much as possible about
Calcutta's prison system. What he found was a regime corrupt to
the very core, where anything could be bought, or done, for a price.
One of the first things to catch Jack's attention was prison food. It
was not so much that the diet of puffed wheat and water or chick-
peas and rice was inadequate; rather that prisoners were not
provided with any containers from which to eat this meagre fare.
Many would use banana leaves, although this inevitably led to
spillage. Those without friends or relatives to provide containers
simply went without.

Jack soon obtained something to eat out of; his friends saw to
that. But even the well-connected were obliged to use one latrine,

situated at the end of one of two adjoining cells occupied by some eighty men.

> It stank to high heaven day and night. There had been a proper toilet there some years ago, in the days of the British. But all the plumbing had been taken out and what I found was just a tin of water with which to wash yourself after defecation. And some-times getting a tin was no easy thing. Of course you also needed a water container with which to wash yourself, and since these were somewhat scarce commodities you often ended up washing in unfiltered river water, which was highly polluted and the equivalent of washing in raw sewage.

Jack's supporters, led by voluntary worker Frances Meigh, im-mediately set about the urgent task of securing his freedom, and within eight days they had done so. But eight days in an Indian prison also meant eight nights, and, as the doctor soon discovered, the hours of darkness were scarcely conducive to sleep. Once prisoners had been locked in their cells, from the late afternoon onwards, all manner of criminal activities got under way. The convicts who ran the cells would play cards and smoke hashish; homosexuality was encouraged by leaving convicts in charge of other prisoners for twelve hours nightly. There was not a single guard to prevent any of this illicit activity in the cells, in which there were forty men packed together on the floor, with little room to turn.

Nor were the efforts of Frances Meigh going well. A Mr Bruce, the Second Secretary at the British High Commission in Calcutta, usually a person whose help could be relied on, was apparently unavailable. The High Commission was closed, the staff having taken the day off to celebrate the wedding of Prince Charles to Lady Diana Spencer.

While the pageantry of the Royal Wedding unfolded in St Paul's in London, the prison doctor's assistant at Alipore Jail (himself a convict) was seeking Preger's advice about an ulcer on his penis. He admitted to having had anal intercourse with a male prisoner and asked if Jack might be able to arrange for penicillin to be sent into the prison for him. He claimed that the Alipore doctor would not supply the necessary injections, so Jack approached the head jailer to check his story. In fact the prison doctor had been ordering and receiving 200 vials of penicillin per month. Since the number of inmates was about 4,500, this meant that the prison doctor was diagnosing and treating one to two hundred new cases of venereal disease every month. Jack explains:

> In other words, the prisoners weren't getting this medicine. Nor did they need it. The drugs were just being misused. You see, the prison guards demanded a share of every single thing that went into that prison. It was all one big racket.

By the time Jack's case came to court, Frances Meigh had persuaded the Indian Red Cross to certify that they needed the doctor's skills. And then her trump card: a testimonial to Jack's work from a rather special source. It was read out to the court:

> To whom it may concern:
> I have seen the work of Dr Jack Preger in Bangladesh and what I saw was very good for the people and the children. I do hope he will be able to give that same service to the needy here in Calcutta also.
> In my prayers for him.
> God bless you.
> Mother Teresa.

Some of the solicitors whose help Frances Meigh had enlisted rose to their feet. While the atmosphere in the courtroom remained electric, her lawyers incorporated the sentiments of both the Indian Red Cross and Mother Teresa into a plea couched in suitably Calcuttan legalese:

> And the petitioner prays for bail and there is no chance of him absconding or evading trial, if he is enlarged on bail for the sake of the poor community, and those who are deprived of proper treatment.

The judge himself was swept along by the tide of emotion. 'Bail granted,' he announced without the slightest hesitation. The entire hearing had taken less than twenty minutes.

One consequence of Preger's brush with the Indian penal system was still to reveal itself. For immediately after his liberation he developed amoebic dysentery, a serious medical condition. It was to take three courses of treatment and four and a half months to cure. As he prescribed his own medication the doctor was in no doubt: his illness was entirely attributable to the filthy water supply. Often, during those painful months, Jack was unable to walk more than a few yards, as a result of a combination of stomach cramps, weakness and extreme fatigue.

> The best thing about coming out of prison was to be able to be in the open air again – away from the terrible stench of drains. Because you can shut out most things from your mind – the corruption, the beatings, the whole rotten prison system – but you just can't get rid of the smell of sewage. That was with you, day and night and, believe me, it's bad.

The first thing Jack did was to return to Alipore, but now with visitor status only. It was for a specific purpose. Having befriended a prisoner whose clothes were in tatters from a round of beatings by the police, Jack returned to the prison and gave him a set of clothes from his own modest wardrobe. Of course the prison guards had to be persuaded to turn a blind eye to this. In Calcutta's jails, however, almost anything can be arranged.

As Jack continued to recover from his ordeal, he began to compare his own sorry state with that of Calcutta's most famous resident, and unofficial saint, Mother Teresa. Since her letter of support had been well received by the court, he had every reason to be grateful to her. Nevertheless, despite his initial admiration, he has long been one of her fiercest critics.

Although, like Mother Teresa, he was dedicated to helping the poorest of the poor, Jack was now poised to embark on a series of protracted legal battles with the West Bengali authorities. By contrast, Mother Teresa's life of self-sacrifice had long been the focus of world recognition, culminating with the award of the Nobel Peace Prize in 1979. While Preger was continually at loggerheads with the Catholic Church of Calcutta, the Pope was able to find in Mother Teresa a living example of the rejection of those materialistic values that the Vatican believes have so corrupted the modern world. And whereas Preger was battling hard for the right merely to remain in India in order to run a modest street clinic for destitutes, the Nobel laureate could point to well over twenty homes for the dying, the sick, and lepers that she had established throughout the city.

If the British doctor is a little jealous of her success, it is not surprising, for on the face of it there is much common ground between them. Both are foreigners who have championed the rights of the poor and oppressed of Calcutta, and both have been profoundly influenced by the Catholic faith. Preger might well have been accused of being an Israeli agent or a member of the CIA, but neither has Mother Teresa been immune from the wrath of many a Calcuttan during her long career. Nor could Preger take issue with her unique interpretation of Christ's message, which she has so eloquently expressed:

> Be kind and merciful. Let no one ever come to you without coming away better and happier. Be the living expression of God's kindness. Kindness in your face, kindness in your eyes, kindness in your smile. Kindness in your warm greeting. In the slums we are the light of God's kindness to the poor. To the children, to the poor, to all who suffer and are lonely, give always a happy smile. Give them not only your care, but also your heart.

For several years Jack Preger had been the very embodiment of each and every one of Mother Teresa's impressive injunctions; his work in Bangladesh and Middleton Row were ample testimony to that. Has all that they have in common led to the forging of a formidable alliance? Quite the opposite, for, almost from the outset, their relationship has been characterized by caution and mutual distrust. During the seventies Mother Teresa agreed to hand over a plot of land to Preger. It was a modest smallholding, on a site well away from the squalor of Calcutta, and it was the doctor's intention to convert it into a communal farm. Trained as an economist, experienced as a farmer and qualified as a medical practitioner, Preger was ideally placed to help. Suddenly, Mother Teresa changed her mind and the project was cancelled. No explanation was ever given.

The elderly Albanian had come to Calcutta in 1928, when she was eighteen and known as Agnes Gonxha Bojaxhiu; a good half century before Jack had started to work with the down-and-outs of Howrah. It is not without some irony that her first port of call on arriving in the city was the teaching convent of the Irish Loreto Sisters, situated in Middleton Row. And while Mother Teresa would in later years express admiration for Preger's work, he now finds himself a little reluctant to return the compliment:

I was definitely influenced by Muggeridge's film *Something Beautiful for God*, which described Mother Teresa's work in Calcutta so effectively. And on the occasions when I have met her, I have had the impression that I was in the presence of some kind of a holy person. And there's no doubt that she has served the people of Calcutta well. But there is another aspect of her work about which people remain unaware – for the fact of the matter is that Mother Teresa is prepared to shake hands with any type of murderer who happens to be in political power. For example, when there was a diplomatic reception some two weeks after the coup in Bangladesh, she was there, lining up with the rest of the diplomatic corps and shaking hands with the new people in power – the very same people who had just murdered fifty of their opponents and will no doubt go on killing future opponents. It's the same here in Calcutta. I appreciate that she has now resigned as head of the Order of the Missionaries of Charity, but there's no doubt that she still has the Chief Minister eating out of her hand. That's why she's happy to say that the government is doing such a magnificent job against tremendous odds – when the truth is that all they are doing is constantly turning away from the most incredible human rights atrocities.

If Preger is angry with the tiny octogenarian, it is partly because he regards her work as a series of missed opportunities. The root of this conflict lies in the fact that the Missionaries of Charity is primarily a praying order, not a medical establishment. The emphasis on the power of prayer is thrown into particularly sharp relief at Nirmal Hriday, Kalighat, Calcutta's celebrated home for the dying, founded by Mother Teresa. She insists that the needs of the unfortunates occupying the beds of Kalighat are met in full:

> Nobody in our home in Kalighat has died depressed, in despair, unwanted, unfed or unloved. That is why I think this is the treasure-house of Calcutta. We give them whatever they ask, according to their faith. Some ask for a prayer. We try and give them whatever they want.

Yet if it is medication that they want, their request is less likely to be favourably received. An inspection of the rules and aims of the Order confirms that medical attention to the poor is low on the agenda. The priority is quite clear: the worship of Christ and the propagation of the faith. For this reason the medical interests of patients are not always well served. Certainly no painkillers are administered to patients; belief remains firmly vested in the intervention of the Almighty. And there are examples of medical malpractice at Kalighat that would horrify western observers. For example, needles for injections are simply rinsed in cold water after use and passed on from one patient to the next. And patients with TB are not isolated, despite the highly contagious nature of the disease. Its spread, it is held, is best left in His hands. As one former volunteer has remarked:

> I'm sure that such faith must be admirable, but it is difficult to swallow if you don't share it. The controversy is not that the Missionaries of Charity is essentially a contemplative order – that's fine. But if they want to pray, let them pray and not dabble haphazardly with medicine.

When it came to the maintenance of her own ailing health, Mother Teresa was a little less complacent, and more reluctant to rely on the power of the Spirit alone. She preferred to have the best doctors flown in from overseas, to have a pacemaker fitted by highly skilled heart surgeons, and then to recuperate in the post-cardiac care unit of the Woodlands nursing home, the most exclusive private clinic in Calcutta, and certainly no Kalighat.

Preger is scathing of Mother Teresa's assertion that at the moment of death the destitutes of Calcutta suddenly acquire an inner peace that might previously have eluded them:

You see, it suits the Corporation of Calcutta to have a place like Kalighat, where they can dump many of their destitutes. Many will die there and many will die unnecessarily. Nobody in Mother Teresa's Order would ever dream of turning round and saying, 'My God, why don't they do something about it, why don't they build some homes or start some factories?' – they never say that – they just say how beautifully he or she died. Which is just all nonsense, quite apart from being socially regressive. What actually happens is that when people die they get this contraction of the face muscles called *risus sardonicus* – this sardonic bitter smile – through which you get the teeth coming out and the lips drawn back as if it's a smile. It's this smile that is misinterpreted by Mother Teresa and her novices as some kind of proof that these poor, wretched people were somehow happy when they died.

Antonia Walder is a former volunteer from England who has worked closely with both Preger in Middleton Row and Mother Teresa at Kalighat. In a written report submitted to the company that sponsored her visit, she had this to say about their competing approaches:

Jack and Mother Teresa have frequently come to blows in arguing. Mother has this incredible, unquestioning faith, which Jack cannot accept as an answer to the medical needs of the poor in Calcutta. Both seem to be rather bitter about the other, which is such a shame for two such admirable people who essentially care about the same things and are striving for the same goal.

Whether or not Mother Teresa and Preger share the shame objectives is open to question. Whatever the case, Maritta Preger, Jack's first wife, has another, less charitable, explanation for this lingering rivalry:

> The thing with Jack is that he's always got to be the kingpin. It was a problem for him when, as a child, he used to think that Leslie was the favoured son. It was the same as soon as our son Alun was born – Jack immediately had his nose put out of joint by no longer being the sole object of all attention. Jack always has to be first. That is why he is out there in India now – he has to be out there with his own tribal following – and that's why he isn't too kindly towards Mother Teresa. She is quite clearly the number one, and he doesn't like that one bit.

One fact is beyond dispute: that the work of both Dr Jack and Mother Teresa has obliged them to become intimately acquainted with the reality of death on the streets of Calcutta. Seldom does a day pass without the demise of either an occupant of a Kalighat bed or a patient of Middleton Row. However, Jack now found himself obliged to confront the death of his own mother. Eighty-two years of age and suffering from a terminal illness, Bertha had been stubbornly clinging to life for some time, defying her doctors' predictions. Jack was determined to see his mother for what he was certain would be the last time. It was to be an opportunity to say goodbye. But he soon discovered that bidding farewell to his mother was not going to be as straightforward as he had envisaged. For although Jack remained on bail charged with defying an order to quit India, for which offence he could be jailed for five years or deported if found guilty, the authorities did their utmost to thwart his return trip to England by setting his bail figure at the ridiculously high sum of 500,000 rupees, over £30,000. It was a bizarre example of administrative double-think, a Calcuttan catch-22, and not the first experienced by the doctor.

For Jack, the solution was clear – and it did not lay within the jurisdiction of the law courts: it was time to involve the Press. His experience in Bangladesh had taught him that the international

Press, if exploited effectively, could penetrate where legal arguments before a West Bengali tribunal clearly could not. Once again the *Daily Telegraph* rallied to Jack's cause. A few days after the appearance of its headline £30,000 BOND FOR BRITON TO SEE SICK MOTHER, an Alipore judge drastically reduced the sum.

When Jack arrived in Southport he found that his mother was very ill indeed. A live-in nurse had been hired to attend to Bertha's needs. Anita, the youngest of the three Preger children, recalls that despite her brother's long absence from Jewish orthodoxy, he was extraordinarily sensitive to his mother's feelings:

> I remember that the nurse brought some food in on one occasion for Jack to eat, and she had put some butter on the table with the meat. Of course she wasn't to know the complexities of the laws of the *kashrut* – of how milk and meat have to be kept separately. But this upset Jack – even though he had been a practising Catholic for some years – because he knew that mother wouldn't have liked it. So he refused to eat the meal.

The following year, 1983, Bertha Preger passed away. She died in Anita's arms. The same Yiddish love song, '*Shayn vi di Levona*', with which the young Harold Preger had wooed his future bride during the early twenties, was sung tenderly once again, this time by a loving daughter.

In the meantime Jack had returned to Calcutta, but as soon as he learned of the death of his mother he set off again for England. The funeral placed him in something of a dilemma. Having ceased to be a practising Jew some forty years earlier, he was not quite sure to what extent he ought to participate in the proceedings. In the event a compromise was reached whereby Jack recited the Kaddish, the mourner's prayer, while declining to be 'called up' during the synagogue service held on the Sabbath before his mother's burial.

If Jack appears unduly harsh on Mother Teresa and her Missionaries of Charity, is he able to muster any more enthusiasm or respect for her spiritual leader, His Holiness the Pope John Paul II? When the Pilgrim Pope, as he is popularly known, arrived in Calcutta on 3 February 1986, he proceeded directly to meet Mother Teresa, to whom twenty-one years previously the Vatican had granted a *Decretium Laudis*. This signified approval of her Missionaries of Charity and accepted the congregation as one of pontifical right, so that the Order operated directly under Rome and could work outside India. Jack was not impressed by this close alliance between popes past and present. In fact the visit of His Holiness to India served to loosen still further Jack's tenuous attachment to the Catholic Church.

I went to the Pope's Mass here in Calcutta, and it was horrible. He was staying not far from where I was working, so I went up just to see what he looked like. He had just come back from Kalighat and was travelling on the back of this Landrover in a bullet-proof case – the Pope Mobile. He was all dressed up in full regalia, so he looked like something in a fairground. I remember in Blackpool, on the Golden Mile, there used to be this great big glass case with a clown inside. When you put a penny in, this clown would laugh and laugh and rock about for a couple of minutes – all for the sake of one penny. I had the same sensation looking at the Pope in this incredible glass box. The Pope was on his way to an enormous Mass before tens of thousands of people, but at one point I was the only bystander. Our eyes locked – because he had no one else to look at – and he raised his hand to me.

Did this personal papal salutation represent the apotheosis of Jack's commitment to Catholicism? No, on the contrary, he found the entire situation so absurd that he was quite unable to summon up even a wave in return:

I was just terribly embarrassed by the whole thing. I felt that there was something wrong. It was all such claptrap, pure show business. After the Pope Mobile there followed a single-decker bus in which there were all these cardinals, all leaning out of the

145

windows with their little crosses. Once again there was no one to wave to except me – and I just looked at the whole lot of them in disgust. It was all so stylized and full of pompery.

As Preger grew ever more alienated from the mainstream of Catholicism, so his analysis of the ills of society, both in Calcutta and elsewhere, became increasingly radical. His vocabulary, too, appeared to reflect the rekindling of earlier, leftist tendencies. For in both his writings and conversation there was a good deal less theology and considerably more politics. When Preger emerged from Alipore Special Jail, for example, there was no doubting his anger with 'the system', and he embarked on a limited campaign of penal reform, determined to highlight the primitive prison conditions in Calcutta. He succeeded in arranging a meeting with the Chief Justice in New Delhi, Mr Y. V. Chandrachud, in which the details of his eight-day ordeal were vividly described, and the Chief Minister politely promised swift remedial action. And, writing in the journal *Frontier*, the doctor set out his own radical agenda for prison reform:

> The authorities have to be forced to act. Not by changing the names of buildings, not by switching prisoners around from one pit of iniquity to another. But by overhauling this self-perpetuating capitalist system of graft and corruption which helps the bourgeois establishment in 'Marxist' West Bengal to maintain its position *vis-à-vis* the exploited and brutalized poor.

For Jack the litmus test was human rights. It always had been. He now found himself speaking out in defence of many good causes, ranging from the deplorable number of the non-criminal insane detained in Dum Dum Jail to the plight of the Buddhist Chakma tribes being driven out of the Chittagong Hills by Bengali Muslim settlers. Preger embraced causes that many had not even heard of. 'In Mymensingh District in Bangladesh,' he thundered in another article, 'the Garos have been evicted from their traditional lands and have been driven to claim a Garo reservation which takes no notice of the Meghalaya border.'

It was for the sake of the destitutes of Middleton Row, for the inmates of Alipore, for the lunatics unjustly held in Dum Dum Jail, and for all those whose fundamental human rights were being abused, that Preger became more determined than ever to remain in Calcutta. His work there was still unfinished. Here, then, was the reason why the legal actions against him had to be vigorously defeated. Preger's legal battles would last the best part of a decade and demand of him more than a hundred court appearances. But if any West Bengali official thought that Jack's spirit might easily be crushed, he would have been making a massive error of judgement. In a letter to the Foreign and Commonwealth Office in London, the rebellious doctor set out his credo:

If the West Bengal government pursue their case against me, it is a foregone conclusion that I shall eventually be deported to the UK. What the West Bengal government has so far failed to grasp, is that after deportation I shall seek to raise the return fare in the UK by public appeal and return to Calcutta as soon as possible. I shall then immediately apply for permission to resume work among the destitutes. After returning to Calcutta after deportation, I shall not accept any more quit orders from the West Bengal government and I shall accept imprisonment instead. If I am refused re-entry to India after my return from the UK, I shall seek to enter illegally by land and immediately offer myself to Security Control for re-arrest and trial. The choice is, therefore, between West Bengal permitting me to work with destitutes here and holding me in prison indefinitely. Under the Foreigners' Act I may be imprisoned for up to five years. But I have assured the West Bengal government that after, say, five years in one of their appalling jails I shall, if alive, reapply for permission to work with their poor. And if ordered to leave and then deported, I shall resist such deportation and in any case return illegally.

Preger could hardly have made himself more clear. He would continue to fight, to the death if necessary, for the poorest of the poor of Calcutta. Here was an issue of fundamental rights over which there could be no compromise. But what had happened, during this great campaign, to the fundamental rights of Jack's own wife and children?

9
Embracing Humanity – Losing
a Family

It was not until 1986, some seven years after Jack had set out for Calcutta, that Cathy returned to India. She purchased two airline tickets, both return. One of these was for a pretty, fair-haired six-year-old by the name of Anna. When she boarded the plane bound for Calcutta, the child could scarcely conceal her excitement. It was her first major trip overseas. But Anna was more than just Cathy's enthusiastic travelling companion; she was her daughter. Furthermore, she was soon to be reunited with her father, with whom she had so far enjoyed precious little contact.

Anna was conceived just before Jack's departure for Calcutta during the summer of 1979. Within hours of the time at which his plane was scheduled to leave, Cathy had telephoned her husband at Bertha's house in Southport, to tell him that she was pregnant. For Jack, all set to start work with the destitutes of Calcutta, it was most certainly not good news. The announcement of a new arrival on the eve of his departure was not quite the send-off he had envisaged. As Jack's sister points out:

> Well, its the oldest trick in the book – you come off the pill when your husband is due home. Cathy thought that this would bring Jack home, so baby Anna was quite deliberate in that sense.

149

If Cathy's pregnancy was indeed a ploy to ensure that Jack's stay in Calcutta was short-lived, it was to be entirely unsuccessful. It was perhaps even counter-productive, as Cathy explains:

> Anna was conceived unexpectedly on our last meeting in the summer of 1979. This big misunderstanding arose because Jack thought that I became pregnant deliberately to keep him in England. But he never spoke very openly about this. Therefore I never was invited to live in Calcutta.

As Jack began to attend to the medical needs of the destitutes of Howrah, Cathy's baby continued to grow in the womb. Anna was born in April 1980, although Jack scarcely saw his daughter until Christmas that year, by which time he was a little over fifty. Just as Maritta had earlier insisted that her marriage to Jack had deteriorated almost immediately after their son Alun was born, so Cathy's marriage to Jack all but disintegrated when Anna entered the world:

> From the very moment that Anna was born there was this coldness on Jack's part for such a very long time. I was living in a flat in Norfolk when Jack came to visit us around Christmas time. Of course Anna was still a very small baby, but all he would say is, 'It's a very Victorian baby.' He just didn't want to know.

Since her deportation from Bangladesh, Cathy had been living on a run-down council estate in Norwich, where for the first time in her life she had rubbed shoulders with single-parent families and the unemployed. Since funds from Calcutta were few and far between and family allowance was not enough to make ends meet, Cathy was obliged to return to work when Anna was just nine months old. Although obliged to carry out only the most menial of tasks as an auxiliary nurse, she was nevertheless grateful for the work. For here was an additional source of income, with the all-important perk that she could have Anna with her while she worked. Even so, Cathy still had a list of grievances with a momentum that, in time, would become unstoppable:

By this stage it definitely wasn't a marriage. People would look at me and say, 'Oh, poor you.' But I would reply that I would much rather have a happy husband, someone who is doing what he wants to do. Once some old ladies asked me to speak to them about Jack's work out in India. I started the talk by saying, 'This man is my husband – but I don't really know if I am married to him or not.' And for years it was like that. I think that Jack's expectation was that I would be waiting for him in perpetuity, such was his capacity for self-delusion. But he would give me so little in return. For example, when finally I did make it out to Calcutta – albeit for a holiday with Anna – I asked Jack for one decent photograph of the two of us together – I didn't have one other than our wedding photo. I said that this would help me when I would go back to England; it was something to feed off, if you like. But even for this modest request he simply glazed over – it was really most peculiar, this refusal to give me this very little thing that I wanted. I often used to try to get support for Jack in Norfolk, but never really succeeded. Because people would reply that 'Charity begins at home.' I would retort rather snappily, 'Yes, but it doesn't end at home.' Unfortunately, though, nobody was really ever that convinced by what I had to say. And I have to admit that I did find it quite a constraint in trying to get my husband back that his work was for such a great and noble calling, one in which I basically believed.

As the months of waiting slipped into years of uncertainty, Cathy herself began to share many of the doubts of those who knew her in Norfolk. Although her faith in her marriage was sustained for some time by a Pentecostal group to which she had become attached, Cathy began to wonder if she might not be better off free of Jack. For not only had the long wait been of little avail, but also there appeared to be only the most slender of chances that her husband's quarrel with the Indian authorities would ever be resolved.

Nor did Preger project himself as a partner desperate to salvage or sustain this ailing match. It was he, after all, who had harboured such grave doubts about the wisdom of marrying in the first place. And when in 1987 Cathy returned to Calcutta for a second time, again with Anna, there was that same stony silence on Jack's part when it came to discussing their future together. Every time an opportunity presented itself for Cathy to join her husband in Calcutta, it was hastily vetoed by Jack. The time was not right, the accommodation was unsatisfactory, the court case had still to be settled. An apparently compelling reason was always to hand.

Cathy's needs were hardly complex: she just wanted to be loved. Tired of waiting for her husband to complete his lengthy battles with the chaotic legal system in Calcutta, Cathy finally did what many had been urging her to do for some time: she met another man, a widower by the name of John McGregor. As hesitant as Cathy had been in the past, she now began to move with some decisiveness, divorcing Jack and marrying McGregor.

It is surely reasonable to think Jack would have welcomed this sudden and unexpected liberation from what he saw as the stifling constraints of matrimony. Having argued against the marriage almost from the outset, and having absented himself for several years, surely he had got not just what he deserved, but what he wanted, too.

In fact Jack's reaction was not so predictable. No, now the roles seemed to be reversed, with Jack purporting to be the aggrieved party; claiming that it was he, not Cathy, who had been wronged. Complaining bitterly to Anita, he was adamant that Cathy should have stood her ground a little longer. For on receiving the divorce papers from his wife, he argued that he had been on the very brink of sorting everything out. If only she could have been more patient:

'She needn't have done this, you know,' the newly divorced doctor told his sister, 'because I had just got the money together for them to come out here.'

Free once again, Jack became desperate to regain what had for many years been his for the taking. He even asked if Cathy would marry him again once the decree absolute had been officially granted by the British courts. And when rejection came, as inevitably it did, Jack battled hard with his new status:

I asked Cathy why she married John. And she said that I never provided her with a home – that he had got one and that he would provide for her. John's wife died and he nursed her while she was ill, in spite of his own handicap, and he continued to frame pictures from his wheelchair. So all of this added a gloss of goodness to what she was doing. But in fact what she was doing was abandoning her husband, who was under trial in a foreign country.

The conflict between embracing humanity on the one hand and fulfilling one's obligations to one's family on the other, is entirely avoided by those who have taken a vow of celibacy. Jack's friend Shaemus Cunnane, by this time a canon, explains:

So now you see why we have celibacy for Catholic priests; that when people find something and dedicate their lives to it, then others are less likely to get hurt. I sensed from the outset that a chap with a sense of vocation as strong as Jack's was going to have a very hard time – unknown to himself – and as such he really should never have married. You need a bit of human affection, and it's hell on anyone he marries.

It was not much better for Anna. But whereas Cathy's three children from her first marriage were to grow up entirely deprived of contact with their father, Cathy was determined that Anna would not suffer likewise. In this respect, at least, she has been successful.

Fortunately Anna is a very happy and well-adjusted child. When we were out in Calcutta Anna worked on the streets with Jack – an experience which she enjoyed very much. My view was that whatever my differences with Jack, it's always better to have something positive to hang on to.

Cathy's approach was certainly pragmatic, but for many years young Anna wanted considerably more from her father. Just as Alun, twenty years earlier, had been desperate for his father's love, so Anna would in later years confide that she would much rather have been a little Indian girl 'so that Daddy will love me more'.

While Anna was grappling with the reality of her father's long absences abroad, Jack was preoccupied with the plight of children other than his own. He had not forgotten the fate of those Bangladeshi children who had been abducted from their parents, and in support of whose cause he had been deported from Bangladesh. It was true that Jack had travelled to Calcutta because he had a working knowledge of both the Bengali language and culture. But there had been another reason for his presence there: he considered that the overcrowded capital of West Bengal would be the ideal base from which to pursue his campaign to reunite those missing youngsters with their families. Jack had made a promise to the parents:

> In Bangladesh, I told the parents I would do everything I could to find their children. I couldn't turn round and simply say that it had become inconvenient to help them.

He was as good as his word. For it was in Calcutta that the doctor decided to organize protests against the fraudulent export of Bangladeshi children by the Dutch adoption agency Terre des Hommes, headed by Moslem Ali Khan. For offering *satyagraha*, or non-cooperation as advocated by Mahatma Gandhi, Jack selected the offices of the Bangladeshi deputy High Commission in Circus Avenue, and Bangladesh Biman, the country's national airline, whose offices are very near the street clinic of Middleton Row. His one-man show attracted the notice of the local newspapers, which reported the demonstrations with some interest. These protests were held with the express permission of the police and remained peaceful at all times. On one occasion, however, a policeman from the Park Street station gave a brief speech before disbanding the protest. In his speech he told the small crowd that Jack was an agent of Mrs Gandhi, and that he was protesting against the export of children because he was adamantly opposed to the entry into Britain of additional black babies.

Whatever the ploys of the local police, Jack became convinced that his espousal of the Bangladeshis' cause was inextricably bound up with the campaign by the West Bengali authorities to be rid of him. Here was the driving force behind the constant stream of orders to quit. As Jack continued to fire off angry letters to the Press, to draft articles condemning this authority or that, a clear view of the doctor began to emerge in Calcutta's corridors of power: he was a troublemaker who would have to go.

What of Jack's own son back in England? Alun had been engaged in battles of his own in which, rather like those facing his father, victory could not be taken for granted. Unlike Jack, who was always able to vent his wrath on some particular branch of the powers that be, Alun was engaged in battles of a psychological nature. For his greatest struggle has been with himself. Withdrawn from his earliest days at school, and completely obsessive by nature, Alun saw little of his father during his formative years and has suffered from various mental disorders and nervous difficulties ever since. For many years the pattern was invariably the same, with Alun going from one medication to the next. Sometimes the doctors' diagnoses were correct, at other times they were way off course. Unaware of Jack's conversion to Catholicism or of his entanglements with the Indian authorities, Alun last saw his father in 1983, the year in which Bertha Preger, the grandmother he never saw, had passed away.

Maritta needs no reminding that there has been next to no contact between father and son, but that has not prevented her from detecting striking similarities between them:

The only interest I have in Jack nowadays is when there is a complication with Alun; for then I look to Jack, the mirror-image, to try to see if it might help with my son. Alun has also heard voices and he also cuts himself off from other people, so I do think that there is a strong hereditary factor with these two men. Certainly both are most obsessive by nature. I always thought and hoped that Jack might be able to use his very considerable medical skills to help Alun, his own son, whom he has hardly ever known or seen – but unfortunately it was not to be. I do find it quite ironic, though, that while Jack has ended up working with Indian destitutes on the streets of Calcutta –

people to whom he is entirely unrelated – our son, the son of a British doctor, has on more than one occasion been over-prescribed medication by Indian doctors working here in England.

Meanwhile the government of Bangladesh was forming what it described as a 'high-powered inquiry team' to question the parents at Dattapara, the Dacca refugee camp where forty-one families had mysteriously been deprived of their children. The team was in fact a four-member panel consisting of Dr Mizanur Rahman Shelley and three of his colleagues from the Bangladeshi Directorate of Social Welfare, some of those accused by Preger of carrying out the abductions. Most outrageous of all, Moslem Ali Khan, the man at the very centre of the allegations, was himself allowed to interrogate witnesses during the course of the inquiry. It came as no surprise to Jack when the four-page government report on the case absolved everyone of any wrongdoing and concluded that his allegations were without any foundation whatsoever.

While accusations are flying, has the doctor's own conduct been blameless? Preger is acutely aware that it would not be too taxing to draft a weighty indictment against him. This would not be a dry juridical document, along the lines of those with which the West Bengali authorities have long preoccupied themselves, but an al-together more intimate account:

> That's why I get so intensely embarrassed by all this 'saintly' stuff that keeps getting heaped upon me. I am certainly no saint – nor have I ever been. When people say to me, 'What fantastic work you're doing,' I reply, 'You don't know about my personal life in the past, but you might well be finding out about it in the not too distant future.'

Is this statement of Jack's a reference to those he has left behind in order to be in Calcutta; is he speaking here of Maritta and Alun, of Cathy and Anna? Yes, but not exclusively. For when Cathy was attempting to describe the complex personality of her former husband, she said more than she knew:

> I wouldn't say that Jack is exactly a bottom-pincher, but he does get on extremely well with people, especially all those young girls who go out to work in Calcutta as volunteers.

Cathy was right. Jack had indeed struck up a number of relationships with some of the young and female volunteers of Middleton Row. He reveals this much himself:

> You see, since I've been working in Calcutta I have been involved in three relationships, over a timespan of some six years. The first relationship was OK in the sense that it didn't last very long, but unfortunately in both of the other relationships the two girls, both of them Swiss, absolutely refused to practise any kind of normal birth control. This wasn't for religious reasons – far from it – it was because they wanted to enjoy a certain kind of sexual excitement. Both girls had had lovers before; one had had an enormous amount of lovers before. She had always managed to time her sexual relationships properly, but both girls apparently made errors with their dates. One had become ill and taken some medicine which didn't agree with her. The other one just got a bit mixed up but never worried about it unduly because the 'safe period' method of contraception had previously always worked for her. Anyway, both of these Swiss girls produced little boys – my little boys. As soon as the first girl told me that she was pregnant, I told her that I was sure Cathy was going to divorce me, and asked her if she would like us to get married. She just laughed, saying that it was a ridiculous thing. I also asked the other girl once she had returned to Switzerland, but she never replied to my letter.

The arithmetic is not at all difficult: Preger has fathered four children, three sons and one daughter, by four different women. Two of them were his wives; two were not. Although he apparently offered matrimony with uncharacteristic zeal, there has been even less contact with the two young boys, both of whom are now growing up in Switzerland, than the little granted to Alun and Anna.

So the doctor who spends six days out of every seven working with the sick and needy of Calcutta has his own not insignificant casualty list, longer than many of those who lavish praise on him are aware. But Jack would certainly not be the first great idealist or humanitarian to have neglected or short-changed his own. On the contrary, he is part of a long and distinguished line that includes Mahatma Gandhi, Martin Luther King, John F. Kennedy and various other august leaders of the modern world who aspired to the very highest of ideals but who, we are told, mistreated or abused their wives, women and children.

If Preger is guilty of losing touch with his own offspring, his behaviour has not been inconsistent, for he has done likewise with friends. Even Canon Cunnane has had cause to complain:

> I've no doubt at all that Jack is a person of great worth. But to some extent he is on his own − he is by nature a 'loner', and tends to lose touch with his friends. Quite apart from all his battles with the Indian authorities, this is another reason why I tend to worry about him.

The harshest criticism of all, however, has come from the most unlikely of quarters. For it was Bertha Preger, who, in a conversation with her daughter-in-law shortly before her death, had no hesitation about describing her son as 'heartless'. Aware that her life was shortly to come to a close, she was able to see a common thread in Jack's behaviour to which others, particularly his wives, had been almost completely blind. Perhaps the reason for this was that she too had been left behind, even if mainly because of her own prejudices. Whatever the case, her earlier prediction to Cathy could hardly have been more accurate.

'For you,' Bertha had told her daughter-in-law, 'the pleasure is going to be in bringing up the baby.'

As Cathy explains:

She knew precisely what her son was like — she could see the writing on the wall — and I have to say that although it was a message which I wasn't happy to hear at the time, she was absolutely right.

Preger has not entirely escaped the criticism that he has obligations other than to the destitutes of Calcutta, obligations that he has failed to meet. There was a time, not so long ago, when such arguments certainly made an impact on him:

Cathy's mother used to say to me, 'Why did the two of you ever get married, because my daughter's stuck in England?' And her father used to send me beautifully composed letters arguing that I should come home and work in the field of human rights. I did think about this and even applied to join Amnesty International in London. I handed the application in because there was a stage when I really couldn't see any future working in Calcutta. But when I returned on one occasion to West Bengal it was in the middle of a malaria epidemic, and I took a malaria patient off the street up to Premdaan — one of Mother Teresa's homes — in a taxi. I treated her and then took her up there to convalesce. She was very ill indeed — cerebral malaria in many cases here can be a real killer — and as we went up there, she'd known me for a long time, as a destitute who had been a patient on and off for a long time, and she just put her hand on my knee, she didn't say anything — she couldn't. I know this sounds rather like pure schmaltz, like Malcolm Muggeridge on Mother Teresa, but for a woman in this society to put her hand on a male foreigner's knee, well it really is something for a pavement-dweller to do. And I just felt, God, if I wasn't here — if I hadn't treated her — well, she would almost certainly have died there and then on the street. And goodness knows how many others as well. So I wrote to Amnesty and withdrew my application. Now if you try to work out where your priorities lie, or where your justifications lie, it's impossible. Because I find it so difficult to abandon the patients and just go home, which I could do. So I have decided that I really ought to stay here and battle it out.

Jack has been battling it out ever since. But there has been a regular stream of other pressures, in addition to those exerted by Cathy and her family. Because for many years now, Leslie has been quietly urging his younger brother to draw his long-standing commitment to Calcutta to a close.

I think it's reasonable to devote a chunk of your life to looking after the underdog, but to embrace the whole of mankind on your shoulders alone is somewhat destructive. This becomes to the detriment of those around that person – wives and children most especially – although I have to say that to sit in judgement on it is to sit in judgement on progress. I must say that I do feel on very shaky ground here, because I'm not driven as Jackie is. But to some extent my admiration for all of Jackie's good work is tempered by my knowledge of those left behind. That was why I used to take Alun out every now and then when he was a little boy – I didn't like to see any kid without a father, let alone my nephew. How one can measure all of these things against the tremendous work he has done for the poor, I really do not know. But I do think that the highlights of his life are probably accentuated by his admitting to the wayward things that have happened to him, just as many of the saints and prophets did. He has to accept the way he has behaved towards his families, and, to a lesser extent, towards his mother. We've had several rows about this. I feel that he's done enough, that it's now time for him to look after himself and his own family. But Jack has replied that if he didn't do this work then nobody else would, and again I have to admit that there is a certain amount of truth in this. At least Jack does realize that there is a rather ridiculous side to all of this. You know, 'What's a nice Jewish boy like you doing in Middleton Row?'

If Jack Preger's behaviour as a father and husband has been less than first-class, is he able to claim a more impressive record in relation to his long-running campaign on behalf of the missing Bangladeshi children? Had his deportation, or the spate of publicity that followed, led to anything tangible at all? Here, at least, there has been a measure of success. For Preger's dogged protest led to the imprisonment for three years on corruption charges of Abdul Bari, formerly the Bangladeshi Minister for Social Welfare, and the man who sanctioned the 'adoptions'. And it led to the resignation of Dr Mizanur Rahman Shelley, the Bangladeshi Director of Social Welfare. Although Moslem Ali Khan, formerly the Director of Terre des Hommes, was arrested and charged with similar offences, he was acquitted for lack of evidence, principally because Preger was prevented from testifying against him.

In June 1982, moreover, the Bangladeshi Government began to act, imposing more rigorous surveillance on foreign voluntary organizations operating in that country. And in a direct response to the adoptions racket first exposed by Preger, a new and more exacting government ordinance came into effect. Publication of this ordinance was accompanied by the distribution of a government document that alluded to the forty-one families who had been defrauded of their children at Dattapara camp: 'Many children have been taken away from the country,' it affirmed, 'with the pretence of being adopted by families, but in reality they have been criminally used for immoral earnings and gains.'

As for the missing children themselves, alas little has changed. Despite the intervention of the Commonwealth Secretariat, the Anti-Slavery Society, the Minority Rights Group and Interpol, no child ever succeeded in finding its way back to its anguished parents in Bangladesh. For Jack Preger, of course, the battle goes on. But since it is well over a decade now since the scandal was first uncovered, many of these particular children are no longer minors.

In relation to Jack's own missing children, however, Cathy is convinced that he is the one who has come off worse, because he has missed out on enjoying a family. But Cathy's apparent acceptance and adjustment were not achieved overnight. While her marriage to McGregor, a kindly and sensitive man, has helped her, there remains a legacy of anger and frustration towards Jack, not least because of his continuing neglect of Anna. Yet does Cathy really have legitimate cause to complain? Certainly she could hardly have spelled things out more clearly in her presumptuous letter to Maritta almost a quarter of a century earlier. True, she was still in her teens at the time of writing, but her understanding of Jack had been quite acute:

> He thinks that tied to Alun and you he would be weakened, not by the responsibility, but in his purpose and its ultimate fruition. At this point it would be useless to explain that Jack is no good as a father. You will simply have to tell Alun that Daddy has other things to do, lots of sick people to look after.

Cathy had hit the nail on the head. Only now she is obliged to explain to Anna what she had once urged Maritta to explain to Alun. It is a reluctant message, laced with sadness: Jack is no good as a father.

10

Moving Mountains

The Eden maternity ward of the Calcutta Medical College Hospital was once a leading institution not just in India but the whole of Asia. Patients travelled from far and wide in order to benefit from its extensive facilities. Its reputation was second to none. Today it is a shambles. Even the most elementary concepts of hygiene are disregarded. Operating theatres are no longer disinfected. The same catheters are used to clean the respiratory tracts of any number of different babies. Disposable syringes are reused repeatedly on the wards. Until recently, all three heaters needed to maintain the correct room temperature inside the nursery were out of order, producing the perfect breeding ground for infection. In sharp contrast to the hospital's more glorious era, most of its patients are now from the poor and lower middle classes of Calcutta. Three or four mothers are often to be found sharing the same bed, competing for a tiny patch of mattress as they huddle together with their babies. Not surprisingly, something had to give. In July 1989, more than twenty babies developed infections of the skin, respiratory tract and urinary tract. All of them died.

And yet for over a decade now the government of West Bengal has consistently claimed that its medical facilities are adequate, sufficient to meet the health requirements of most Calcuttans, including the city's vast army of the poor. One implication of this complacency is very clear: that offers of additional medical help, free or otherwise, are quite simply surplus to requirement and liable to be refused. It is a restriction that applies as much to major international charities such as Save the Children as it does to an individual practitioner of medicine like Jack Preger. Many charitable organizations have received the government's message loud and clear, and have diverted their energies elsewhere. Jack Preger has not. Jack is the first to admit that the current State Minister of Health, Prasanta Sur, is less than enchanted with him and his work:

I went along to see Prasanta Sur once, when he was Minister of Urban Development, and before he got his present job. I was working in slum areas, and I wanted formal permission from him to work there. He told me that everything was fine in Calcutta and that the city had enough medical facilities. I said that the city most certainly did not, and invited him to come with me and see my patients and their various conditions. He didn't take me up on this invitation, and replied instead, 'Well, if there is anything wrong, then it's the fault of your people, the British. And why don't you go home and look after your own poor for Mrs Thatcher?'

I also went along to see Prasanta Sur, once, armed with a fairly good recommendation from the head of the Lutheran world service, which was spending gigantic sums of money in West Bengal, and had been dealing with Sur on an enormous scale. Well, he just ripped up this chap's reference recommending me and threw it in the wastepaper basket. He said to me, 'You don't have police permission to work here, and therefore I can't talk to you.' And that was the end of that.

And it might well have remained so had it not been for a chance meeting between two Britons in a luxurious outdoor swimming-pool situated near the centre of Calcutta. For during the early part of 1988, a British paediatrician, Dr Sarah Sallon, had taken some time off from her secure job in Israel in order to work on Middleton Row with Jack. Although staying in rather more modest accommodation, she regularly swam at the Oberoi Grand, one of the most stylish hotels in the whole of Bengal. And it was while relaxing in the hotel's elegantly landscaped pool that Dr Sallon made contact with Allen Jewhurst, an independent film producer and a director of the Leeds-based company Chameleon Television Ltd. Jewhurst and his team had just returned from shooting a mountaineering film in Bhutan. As Dr Sallon told Jewhurst about Preger's pioneering work with the street destitutes of Calcutta, and of his long-running battles with the authorities of West Bengal, the television man could scent that here were the makings of a first-class documentary. Accompanying Sallon to Middleton Row, Jewhurst was at once deeply impressed with Preger, and convinced that he had had the good fortune to encounter a living saint. Having made a private donation to the clinic, Jewhurst returned to England, where he embarked on a successful campaign to persuade Channel Four to finance his film.

The producer returned to Calcutta with an undercover crew, and with Sallon duly in place as medical adviser, made the documentary programme '34 Middleton Row: the Jack Preger Story', which was broadcast by Channel Four in April 1988. Sarah Sallon recorded her impressions thus:

> We talked this morning about the morality of making the film, of spending more than $100,000, enough to feed the whole clinic with three meals a day for a lifetime, enough to treat all the TB and leprosy patients for several lifetimes. But Allen is looking for 'emotive issues' to jerk the viewers back home into life, to keep those fingers from the change-channel button. Don't turn over yet, Madam, there's tiny Shakindra, a bag of bones, hanging on to life in the street with all the tenacity of a three-month-old. There's the 'elephant man' who, in a city with so many deformed beggars, hobbles around without covering his face, so terribly deformed. And poor little Rachi whose tubercular cough will push her into the next world if someone doesn't treat her soon. But will they, despite the beatific Jack, skeletal Shakindra, the elephant man and little Rachi . . . still say, 'Turn over'?

Some viewers did switch channels. But millions more did not. The documentary showed the state of Calcutta's decrepit civic services, the medieval government-run hospitals, and then juxtaposed them with views of the five-star facilities of rich private clinics such as the Belle Vue Nursing Home, before finally homing in on Preger's pavement clinic. It also focused on the doctor's predicament: the deportation threat then hanging over him, and the constant harassment by government authorities.

The programme caused a predictable flutter in England. A small group of Britons, awed by Preger's work and indignant at the Indian government's treatment of him, petitioned the Indian High Commission in London. Several British newspapers ran features, the *Observer* carrying a much-discussed article headlined THE DOCTOR WHO WON'T SHUT UP.

The result of all this publicity was that, love him or loathe him, Preger had become impossible to ignore. And not just in the United Kingdom, for the film was soon broadcast in Ireland, New Zealand, Australia and the United States. The wider the audience, the more letters of protest were dispatched to the various Indian High Commissions around the world. The film was achieving what Jewhurst had intended from the outset: to give added momentum to Preger's campaign to achieve registration in Calcutta. Not that the documentary was a model of impartiality, as Christopher Tookey, the television critic of the *Sunday Telegraph* pointed out at the time:

> The Indian and Bangladeshi governments might reasonably claim that there was no 'balance' in this documentary. It was highly emotive, failed to give the right of reply to the authorities, made no effort to understand the technicalities of Indian law, and pretty much ignored the wider social and political implications of Dr Preger's actions. All of which is true; but this remains the most affecting documentary I have seen this year, about a man more deserving of the Nobel prize than of being broken in an Indian prison.

Allen Jewhurst and Christopher Tookey were not the only ones to be swept along by the work of Jack Preger's street clinic. Tanya Le Flemming Burrow, a secretary living in Auckland, New Zealand, was also profoundly moved by his devotion to the destitutes of Calcutta. Having herself worked for two years with various underprivileged groups in Africa, Miss Le Flemming Burrow was able to closely identify with the radical agenda that Jack had set for himself. It was the personal initiative of this young New Zealander that was to turn the tide decisively to Preger's advantage.

Tanya Le Flemming Burrow was in no position to influence things in her own right. But she was most certainly able to do so indirectly. For she happened to be the trusted secretary to Jonathan D. Rose, the managing director of Rose Property Holdings, and a very wealthy man indeed. Flush with profits from numerous speculative land deals, Rose had intended to fund a major programme of health and development in Africa during the mid-nineties. But he was persuaded by his secretary to watch a video recording of Jewhurst's documentary about Preger. One viewing was enough: Africa was off; India was on. Preger was the man to back. This doctor deserved a knighthood, believed Rose, who promptly dictated letters to both the Queen and Mrs Thatcher telling them so. As he packed his bags to fly out to Calcutta and meet this most remarkable man, Rose grew ever more convinced that here was a wrong waiting to be righted.

The property magnate's motives for wanting to help were strictly honourable. In a memorandum to himself recorded on his arrival in Calcutta, he spoke of the reasons why he was prepared to make available a substantial part of his fortune:

> People look everywhere for happiness: in their partner, in their children, in their work, in the amount of money they make, in the possessions they own or will own, in the places they see, in satisfying the opinions of others – but why do they so rarely see that real happiness comes from giving to others? Giving sometimes to the point of your own self-destruction. In some it is a subconscious craving, in others a slow realization that this perhaps is the true meaning of life. President Kennedy put it so pertinently in his inaugural address: 'It is not merely an act of charity that the rich give to the poor; it is a duty.'

Propelled by Kennedy's persuasive rhetoric, Rose did not take long to put his money on the table. It was an offer of staggering generosity: it would henceforth be the policy of Rose Property Holdings to give away at least twenty million rupees, more than £750,000. And that sum was merely the first instalment, for there was a pledge of further monies to follow. In the first instance, ten million rupees were to be allocated to Mother Teresa and the same amount to Preger. Before these considerable sums were injected into the West Bengali economy, however, Rose sought just one concession in return. Preger must be allowed to become officially registered, and thus free to practise medicine in Calcutta. Almost within Jack's grasp was the prize for which he had been campaigning for well over a decade; for which he had been imprisoned in the most appalling of conditions. Here, finally, was the goal that had eluded him for so long.

Jonathan D. Rose was in no doubt that in putting his money on Preger he had picked a winner:

> I believe that, provided he is encouraged, Jack Preger will display abilities vastly superior to those that are just becoming obvious to us. I consider there to be no better person in Calcutta to entrust with both the funds and the lives of these desperate people. We must persist with Jack's problems until they are solved and continue to both fund and encourage him to the point that he gets the success that he so richly deserves. To this end, I must insist that Jack has control over his affairs and will remain perpetually so, in that, in the event of his death, there will be somebody selected by him to continue the work.

Although Rose had still to complete his negotiations with the West Bengali authorities, Jack Preger had every reason to feel more than a little satisfied with himself. His persistent campaigning had paid off. By contrast with his stay in Bangladesh, which had ended abruptly in deportation, his interminable appearances in the courtrooms of Calcutta at last appeared to be drawing to a close. Confident in the knowledge that substantial funding would shortly be flowing his way, Jack began to expand his programme of medical care in the city. Now, still more people could be helped. These moves did not detract from the success of Middleton Row, for its popularity

continued to demonstrate that, despite the government's protestations to the contrary, there remained in Calcutta a profound
gap in the provision of medical services for the poor.

It had never been Jack's intention to make a name for himself as a
street doctor. While at Dublin's Royal College of Surgeons, Jack
had attended not a single lecture in the principles of pavement
medicine. The truth was that he wanted to get away from the paving
stones and canvas of Middleton Row and into a proper building.
Not least because, with drivers speeding around the corner opposite
Loreto House as if the Row was part of a rally course, the possibility
of a patient or pedestrian being run over was becoming more and
more likely. Now, with Rose's backing, he had the opportunity, if
not yet of abandoning Middleton Row, of doing something that
complemented it.

The setting for Jack's second clinic was even more unlikely than
the narrow ribbon of pavement on Middleton Row. For the doctor's choice of site was at Nimtola Ghat, at the side of the Ganges
and next to a cremation jetty. Although an improbable venue for a
clinic, within weeks the stone steps of Nimtola Ghat were being
squatted on by hundreds of Preger's traditional constituents. Not
that the conversion into the Nimtola Ghat Clinic was all that
difficult, for destitutes simply waited on the steps to be examined by
Preger and his growing team of doctors and volunteers.

As the first instalment of New Zealand dollars was converted
into Indian rupees, Preger's third project was launched, with the
opening of a school for more than a hundred poor children. Jack
was doing for the destitutes of Calcutta what Rose had done for the
shareholders of Rose Property Holdings: embarking on a major
programme of acquisition and development. With the government
of West Bengal now promising that registration was merely a
formality that would occur in due course, the unlikely team of Rose,
the man of money, and Preger, the man of medicine, appeared to be
flourishing.

The clinic at Nimtola Ghat was not to survive as long as its sister
clinic at Middleton Row. Local traders began to resent its presence.
It was occupying valuable stall space, they pointed out, especially
during Hindu festivals, when river and sun-worshippers are most

169

likely to purchase any number of religious 'accessories', providing a very lucrative trade indeed. Nor did the occasional flooding of the Ganges help matters. So Jack decided to transfer the site of this second clinic to Patialla Park, a disused park owned by the Corporation of Calcutta and situated on the bank of the Ganges between Howrah Bridge and Nimtola. Where the doctor went, the patients followed.

Middleton Row, Patialla Park and a school for underprivileged children. Were these three centres, devoted to the health and educational care of the poor, enough to satisfy the ambitions of the energetic British doctor? Had Preger now accomplished what he had originally set out to do? Certainly not, for these projects were but the forerunners of still greater things. Preger had not discarded his earlier plans. In fact, his future projects are extensive indeed. Jack is set on establishing mobile clinics for the poor in Calcutta; providing funding for separate rural centres for destitutes suffering from TB, leprosy and other, non-surgical disorders; creating a clinic for destitute psychiatric patients; and buying or leasing land on which to run communal farms in West Bengal on which the destitutes of Calcutta can be rehabilitated and resettled. Moreover, these ambitious plans are quite distinct from the doctor's desire to establish the Mayo Hospital in Calcutta as a medical centre entirely devoted to the care of the dispossessed; and likewise from his long-standing ambition to persuade the government of Bangladesh to take back and resettle on communal farms many of the Bangladeshis who have ended up stranded on the streets of Calcutta.

In the television documentary that she helped to bring about, Sarah Sallon says:

It reminds me a little bit of Moses taking the people back to the promised land. I imagine Jack, in my mind's eye, as a modern-day Moses taking people back over the Hooghly Bridge and back to Bangladesh. He has this dream that they will go back – and that he will go back – and that he will help them make this journey.

This thoroughly modern Moses, however, had still to achieve the more humble status of registration. Shortly before Christmas 1979,

Jack had written to Father Cunnane, 'I hope to get government permission to start a proper programme, but these things take time.' They do indeed. For at Christmas 1989 Preger was still negotiating with the authorities, both judicial and administrative, of West Bengal about his precise status in Calcutta. More encouragingly, there was no doubt that both Jewhurst's film and Rose's finance were having a catalytic effect on Jack's case.

It was as well that Rose's business acumen and determined negotiating skills appeared to be paying off at last. For, unlike Preger, always loath to compromise on an issue of principle, Rose was a pragmatist whose contacts with high-ranking government officials seemed to be removing one stumbling block to registration after another. Having shuttled back and forth to Calcutta, he was soon able to report that:

. . . the meeting with Mr B. K. Saha, the Commissioner of Police, went very well. Everything off the record, he stated that he had no objections to Dr Preger staying, that he did not see him as a security risk, that it was just poor communication and that it would be 'awkward' to cancel the proceedings against him, and that it would need the blessing of a higher power. He said: 'We would not stand in the way if we got that order.' This augurs very well for Jack and necessitates a meeting with Jyoti Basu, the Chief Minister of West Bengal, who is the only one who could give such authority.

Suddenly, things were beginning to happen and, by Calcuttan standards, with astonishing rapidity. On 3 November 1989, Jack was summoned to the office of the Deputy Commissioner of Security Control in Calcutta, where he was informed that the Ministry of Home Affairs in New Delhi had decided to issue him with a visa and was prepared to permit him to work on a permanent basis in the city. Then, on 4 May 1990, the government of West Bengal finally withdrew its charges against Preger, and the relevant magistrate duly acquitted the doctor. The next step, now surely only a matter of weeks away, was registration.

That was the good news. The bad news was that just as the

creaky door of Calcuttan bureaucracy was at last opening to Preger, so another door began to close in his face. Unbeknown to them, the destitutes of Calcutta were about to be adversely affected by issues that could hardly have been more remote from their everyday lives. For what would harm them so was the intricacies of high finance and complex stock-exchange manoeuvrings. A combination of a world economic recession, high interest rates and litigation losses began to erode the fortunes of Rose Property Holdings. Suddenly there was a stony silence from down under. While the New Zealand businessman retained the belief that it was the duty of the rich to help the poor, the problem was that his own fortunes had slumped quite dramatically. Rose's intervention, designed to end Jack's financial struggles, had brought about precisely the opposite effect. For, foolishly perhaps, Preger had allowed a number of new projects to proceed on the basis of a mere pledge of funds from Rose. In a grim newsletter to supporters, Preger outlined his predicament:

7 March 1990

Dear Friends,
I thank you all for the wonderful support we are receiving for our two clinics and the school in Calcutta. Our current commitments require an expenditure of Rupees 500,000 per month and in addition we have five patients for cardiac surgery in the next few months, which will cost a total of about Rupees 250,000 for the surgery alone. Some fourteen months ago we were promised funding from one commercial concern at the rate of Rupees 500,000 a month for twenty months. But due to changed business conditions this donor has so far only been able to provide a total of Rupees 700,000. And I have just been informed that, for the present, no further funding from that source is available. Our problem is that on hearing of his generous offer, we allowed our clinics to expand, and we set up the school last December. We shall do what we can to reduce the scale of our work. We shall take out of our clinics as many patients as possible who are not in urgent need of care; and we shall try to reduce the scale of benefits provided to the remainder of the patients. We may have

to reduce the number of new patients and postpone some of the surgical operations, where possible.

I ask you all to do what you can to raise funds for our work. Once we achieve registration we can then apply to international agencies for funding and supplies. But until registration we are completely dependent upon your assistance.

Jack Preger

Who are these 'friends' to whom this rather desperate plea for help was addressed? In the United Kingdom, support comes in the shape of the Calcutta Rescue Fund, a registered charity run by a small group of volunteers, most of whom have worked with Preger in Calcutta, and in most cases at Middleton Row. A modest pamphlet puts their approach succinctly:

'There are no paid staff, no big offices and no big names to help us. We just believe in what Jack is trying to do.'

The volunteers of the Calcutta Rescue Fund have become an effective lobbying group, constantly in touch with the Indian High Commission in London, attempting to coax and cajole its officials in some way, in addition to their role as a fund-raising unit. Their self-imposed mission to increase public awareness about Jack's work was given a powerful boost by Allen Jewhurst's documentary. Before the programme's transmission the group was run on a shoestring, sending only about £500 to Calcutta in 1988. The following year, however, saw their income increase two-hundredfold, with almost £100,000 sent to Middleton Row. There are hopes of still greater sums to come as the organization becomes more established.

Calcutta Rescue's mailing list has expanded in a similar fashion. Before the film only fifty people were following the work of Dr Jack. After television exposure all that changed, the figure soaring to over three thousand. All over Britain small networks of Preger support groups have sprung up. While the declining fortunes of Jonathan D. Rose seriously undermined the finances of Middleton Row for some time, Jack managed to ward off serious cut-backs in his work with a vigorous programme of jumble sales, church fêtes, raffles and sponsored swims. And it was from funds raised by a group in Sutton Coldfield, England, that the school in north Calcutta, with more than one hundred pupils, managed to maintain its ambitious programme, as well as feeding the children twice daily.

The Preger support movement is now truly international. In December 1986 another registered charity was created, Calcutta Espoir (Suisse), and it is this Swiss organization that is responsible for generating the greater part of Preger's funds. There are now groups all over the world: in Ireland, Spain, France, Germany, Belgium, the United States, Canada and Australia. Naturally some countries generate more funds and publicity than others. But they all endorse the simple slogan of the original, British group: they believe wholeheartedly in what Jack is doing.

It was not long before the government of West Bengal began to seek to impose certain restrictive conditions on Preger. If the doctor was indeed to be 'rehabilitated', then this was to be strictly on their terms. The 'Doctor Who Would Not Shut Up' would have to learn to do precisely that. Without doubt, the government of West Bengal had been badly shaken by Jewhurst's campaigning film. 'Dr Preger will have to undertake,' an official letter insisted, 'never again to be involved in India in any documentary film without specific permission from the government of India or the government of West Bengal.'

And then, for an authority that had long denied any link with the doctor's long-running campaign on behalf of the missing children of Bangladesh, the insertion of a most unlikely clause: 'Dr Preger is not to use India as a platform for indulging in propaganda against Bangladesh or any other country.' Having single-handedly taken on virtually every department in Writers' Building, the government's offices in Dalhousie Square, and on the brink of having beaten the bureaucrats at their own game, was Jack prepared to comply with such terms? There were certainly several compelling reasons for doing so; among them: it would be for the greater good of the clinics, and it would be in the best interests of the lepers and destitutes of Calcutta. Had the doctor finally learned the art of compromise? His reply to the Deputy Commissioner of Security Control answers that question:

I undertake not to use India as a platform for indulging in propaganda against Bangladesh or any other country, but I do not consider as propaganda against Bangladesh requesting a Dutch organization in Bangladesh to pay compensation to the parents at Dattapara Camp, Tongi, near Dacca, for the children allegedly removed by fraud from these parents.

With battles being conducted on a number of different fronts, it is perhaps not difficult to see why a considerable amount of Jack's time, when not at the clinics of Middleton Row or Patialla Park, is spent drafting letters to the various arms of government of West Bengal. These administrative chores are not carried out in a lush suite of executive offices, but at an overcrowded desk in the single rented room in which Preger lives. For quite some time this was in Kyd Street, barely five minutes' walk from Middleton Row. Kyd Street has for many years been the haunt of drug peddlers, pimps and poor Anglo-Indian families. It is therefore not surprising that when Rose visited Preger there he was a little taken aback by what he saw, as an extract from his recordings makes clear:

Jack Preger is in Middleton Row working when I meet him. I later came to see where he lived — a rickety whore-house, the last place in the city, I was told, that would accept him. Everything here is demolition material, and Jack's place was worse than most. Sure as hell he still has his sense of humour, which I would wonder whether I would still retain after sixteen years of living in these conditions.

Rose was so baffled by Jack's choice of living conditions that he took up the matter with the man whose projects he was at that time poised to finance. Rose's transcript reads:

Jonathan How do you put up with all this yourself — you know, the hours you work, and the conditions you work under. How come you're living in something that's been described as a semi-brothel?

Jack   Well, it's next door to a fully fledged brothel.
Jonathan   And how do you personally handle that, Jack?
Jack   Well, I just take care which door I go into at night.

Rose was right. Preger sure as hell retains his sense of humour; an effective safety-valve for coping with many of the traumas of life in Calcutta. The pavements of Middleton Row, the cafés of Park Street and even the musty courtrooms of Bankshall Street have become the daily contours of Jack's rather solitary life. But while his living quarters have habitually been situated in the seedier parts of town, they have nonetheless always been tiny oases of culture. The visual arts have long been Jack's favourite recreation, although many of the BBC's high-quality productions naturally take some time to find their way to West Bengal. When, for example, Dennis Potter's 'The Singing Detective' was screened in India, Jack was enthralled, finding it both revelatory and inspirational.

With the music of Vivaldi often gently playing in the background, Jack has spent countless evenings reading, devouring as always the novels of Hardy, digesting the contents of the latest edition of *The Lancet* or the *British Medical Journal*, ploughing through the *Guardian Weekly*, enjoying the mischief contained in the satirical fortnightly *Private Eye*, shredding magazines into any number of press cuttings that might be of interest to various people; or, perhaps most relaxing of all, quietly puffing away at the small quantity of tobacco neatly packed into his favourite pipe. With the clinics closed on Sundays, Jack is often seen beating a hasty retreat towards an area to the south of Calcutta, where there are a number of lakes, and where the air is a good deal fresher than in the heavily polluted and overcrowded city centre.

'There's no doubt about it,' Jack is now proud to announce, 'I'm definitely an oddball.'

Not sufficiently odd, though, to prevent his writing a series of penetrating articles and book reviews, in addition to a short play. A regular contributor to the left-leaning magazine *Point Counterpoint*, Preger savaged Dominique Lapierre's international bestseller about Calcutta, *The City of Joy*:

The idea is to show that human nature, the spirit of the *bustee* dwellers, will triumph over all adversity. Especially if guided by a Catholic priest. If you accept Lapierre's message, you contribute to the leper children's charity, whose address is given on the cover of the book. The tragedy of Lapierre's approach to these social problems of Howrah, Calcutta or wherever is that if you reject his methods and assumptions, you may well refuse to become involved in any solutions to the real problems. If only Lapierre could be persuaded to limit himself to basic description, he would be outstanding as a social commentator. In five pages on the dumping ground at Dhapa, he says it all. But it is Lapierre's refusal to limit his imagination which reduces his powerful writing to nonsense.

With the government of West Bengal only beginning to recover from the shock of Jewhurst's covertly filmed documentary, it came as no surprise when, in October 1989, permission was denied to the French director Roland Joffé to make the screen version of *The City of Joy* in Calcutta. Preger and the West Bengali authorities at last appeared to have found common cause, albeit from different perspectives, for both disapproved of Lapierre's standpoint.

Jack's lifelong tendency to manic depression persists, although he is now at least able to identify its tell-tale signs, the extreme swings of mood that are often quite unrelated to external events. When Jack is up, though, he is very much up, and the celebrated 'Pregorian sense of humour', as his Oxford soul-mate John Justice once described it, is as active as ever. In fact Jack's mischievous sense of fun has not helped his cause. He was often to be seen sporting a false moustache, by which means he hoped to embarrass the detectives assigned to follow him, and he has in the past sent himself stool samples through the post – to be opened by those whose duty it was to observe the doctor's every movement.

In a prank reminiscent of his Oxford days, Jack once collaborated with a talented artist working in Bengal, who was able to produce an impeccable replica of Mother Teresa's own fair hand. A Christmas card ostensibly from the Nobel laureate herself was sent to Malcolm Muggeridge, for many years a devotee. He was so thrilled to have been remembered by her in this way that he promptly auctioned her card, giving the proceeds to a local charity. In fact Jack's practical joke had been so effective that it was agreed that the most satisfactory course of action was to let matters rest at that. Since this was hardly the original intention of the conspirators, it might well be asked who had the last laugh.

What of the argument that, with the value of Preger's work becoming increasingly acknowledged around the world, the rebel doctor has, in a peculiar reversal of roles, himself become part of Calcutta's establishment? Numerous wars of attrition waged with the bureaucrats of Bengal testify to the fact that he has not. Nonetheless, the language of many Indian journals and magazines suggests that Preger is most certainly held in high esteem. According to the *Illustrated Weekly of India*, for example, Jack is 'one of the twenty-five people who make Calcutta India's most exciting city'. And, in a memorable spelling mistake, the New Delhi publication, the *Sunday Mail*, was proud to dub Preger 'A Schvitzer in the Making'. Apart from being unable to spell Schweitzer, the unfortunate journalist was clearly unaware that in Yiddish a *schvitzer* is someone with a perspiration problem. Almost everybody, it now seems, approves of and applauds Dr Jack.

Leaving aside his work, for the moment, what of Jack's continuing commitment to Catholicism? The truth is that it has not been much in evidence during recent years. In fact, by the autumn of 1989, he was limbering up to a final break with the faith, as he explained in a letter to a friend:

> I'm as much in *shtuch* with my Catholicism as Graham Greene is with his. But really it's all a voyage of discovery, cradle to grave and beyond. No harm, necessarily, in going into a church one year and coming out again (partly) half a lifetime later. Anyway, churches may go one way, individual members another.

The following year Jack was ready to dispense altogether with any lingering attachment to the faith to which he had been so eager a convert. One piece of theology, deemed wholly unsatisfactory by the doctor, was sufficient to accomplish that task. In a letter to a close friend he explained his disillusionment:

> An *Instruction on the Ecclesial Vocation of the Theologian* by Cardinal Ratzinger, and approved by the Pope, has finally pooped my membership of the Catholic church. In at Vatican II and twenty-five years later out with this piece of galloping infallibility.

When Preger finally and firmly shut the door on Catholicism, did this mean that his commitment to and inspiration from the Holy Spirit had likewise ceased? After all, it has been the Paraclete, more than any other single factor, that for decades has sustained the flames of Preger's inner fire in Bangladesh, Alipore Special Jail, Middleton Row and beyond. In fact the power of the Paraclete remains constant in Jack, perhaps more so than ever. As he writes in the unpublished foreword to Frances Meigh's book about him:

> If there is a 'secret' about this work among the destitutes of Bangladesh or Calcutta, it is emphatically an open secret, open to all. It may be expressed in terms of 'revolution' or 'liberation'; but it would be nearer the truth to express it in terms of 'meditation'. It is an opening of oneself to the workings of the Holy Spirit. And for me there is no vagueness about this concept whatsoever. However we may organize our theology, for me the reality is the Paraclete. It is for me not a matter of belief, but of experience.

And in a coded reference to Maritta and Alun, to Cathy and Anna, and perhaps to others too, Preger concludes:

> It is the Paraclete who brought me to where I am. The mistakes I have made, am making and shall make, are my own mistakes. But it is the Paraclete who takes the good element and makes sense of the fly-over people, the street destitutes, and all that has gone before.

With Preger retaining his belief in the power of the Holy Spirit, the divinity of Christ and the Virgin Mary, and with a similar conviction about the intercession of Saints, it is clear that the influence of more than a quarter of a century's Catholic theology was not to be washed away quite so easily. It might be said that a little bit of Catholicism remains, although at some remove from the formality of the established Church, particularly that of Bengal.

'And there's still a little bit of Marxism there in me too,' Preger is proud to announce. Uncle Lazzy, fighter in the Spanish civil war and hero of Jack's boyhood, would no doubt have approved of his nephew's continuing commitment to the principles of the left, despite the recent fall from grace of almost all the world's communist regimes.

Is it possible to add to this unusual *mélange* a little bit of Judaism too? For as the American anthropologist Professor Barbara Myerhoff has pointed out, 'being Jewish comes up in you from the roots'. And since Preger's roots were firmly planted in orthodox Judaism, and since several of his most formative years were spent within the walls of the Manchester Yeshiva, do those roots still survive? In fact Jack's Judaism, although given scant time and attention for almost half a century, remains a key component of both his personality and his motivation.

I can't go along with Jewish teachings towards Christ and Christianity, but as I get older I feel as if I am becoming more Jewish again. It's almost as if the wheel has turned full circle. I still receive Jewish New Year cards from both my brother and sister, and I'm always delighted to receive them. In fact that really means more to me now than Christmas. I don't really know that much about it now, but I'm sure that the Ru'ah ha-Kodesh is not a million miles removed from my understanding of the Paraclete. Jews do have a long history, especially in the Soviet Union, of being active on issues of human rights, and I like to feel that I come from this tradition of Jewish radicalism, and that I'm following it through. The fact of the matter is that you can't just leave your Jewishness behind you. I am only a Christian in the sense that I happened to have joined a Christian organization –

the Catholic Church – at one stage. But I am a Jew and Christ was a Jew. And I'm just trying to follow some of his teachings.

The theological debate is not always easy to follow. There is no such difficulty, however, when it comes to Jack's taste buds. These remain distinctly Jewish. The doctor has spent many an hour chatting with Norman Nahoum – one of under a hundred Jews now to be found in Calcutta – at his celebrated bakery shop in the New Market, discussing the delights and intricacies of Jewish food.

At sixty-one, Jack is thinking about retirement and old age. While both his energy for work and his appetite for a confrontation with this or that authority remain undiminished, the years have nevertheless passed by.

It was my intention to retire at sixty-five, but I've rather slipped behind with my pension payments in the UK. I would love to retire, but I think that what is more likely to happen is that I'll just keep on working until I'm finished. I'd hand over the torch willingly – even if my prospective replacement singed his fingers in the process of receiving it. I've told all of the support groups that it is unwise, in terms of our long-term prospects in Calcutta, to continually place the emphasis on me. It should be on the work. But they do tend to keep on plugging me. I would love to get out of here. This kind of place can drive you round the bend – the working conditions, the living conditions, the corruption and bribery and so on. In fact if I ever did sort myself out and retire, I would love to go somewhere like Jerusalem, or Galilee, where I could study Hebrew and maybe find out more about the historical Christ, which to me is just another part of Jewish history. But I don't expect any of these projects to come off. I think I shall probably just work here until I conk out.

But is there any sign of a younger Preger coming along, someone to whom this bright and bold torch might be handed? The person who has come closest to being that replacement is an Australian doctor, Donald Peters, who has worked in Calcutta for varying lengths of time. A connoisseur of Middleton Row and its environs, Peters has provided free medical care to the street destitutes and lepers of Calcutta on at least six separate occasions over the years, each one spanning a period of several months. By so doing he has jeopardized his more traditional medical career.

Unlike Preger, however, Peters has indicated that he is by no means sure about dedicating his entire life to the poor and oppressed of Calcutta. In fact it recently appeared that the colossal strain of daily life there had been taking its toll on Peters, eroding his enthusiasm for joining Preger in perpetually swimming against the tide. His is the familiar response of feeling ground down by Calcutta, a feeling experienced by many of the volunteers who set out, initially charged with hope, for the pavement clinic of Middleton Row. The Preger support groups scattered across the globe could search high and low. And in time they would doubtless find another medical practitioner, full of the highest ideals, prepared to engage in battle on behalf of others who are often too weak or poor to be able to fight for themselves. But one thing is certain: they will never find another Dr Jack.

Preger's unique contribution to humanity has certainly not persuaded him that, come the Day of Judgement, he will be eagerly received at the pearly gates. Indeed, 'Saint Jack' is convinced that he is going to have a very rough ride:

> I know that in terms of my personal life, my marriages and what's happened to the various children, I've failed. It's all one big mess – and largely of my making. So whatever sorrows I may be going through, I know that I have definitely earned them. In fact I think that I've committed enough sins in my life to merit a fair amount of punishment, which I do believe is going to come to me after my death. Any good that I might have done doesn't intrude on this at all, because to me these are just the kinds of things that one ought to have done anyway.

But is it strictly necessary, in order to be an effective campaigner for human rights, to be prepared to forgo many of one's own basic entitlements, such as the right to family life? For Preger, the answer is quite clear: yes, it is.

In this business of human rights you have got to be prepared to lose everything. You have to be prepared to sacrifice a balanced personal life, you might end up by losing your friends, your family and even your own health. You've got to have people like that, people like me perhaps, who do go over the top – in order to get things done.

Some people approve of this. And some do not. The current Professor of Tropical Medicine at the Royal College of Surgeons, for example, cannot speak too highly of Jack's work:

'The visions of Jack Preger,' the professor is proud to announce, 'should be part of the curriculum of every Irish physician and student in the interdependent world of today.'

For those left behind, however, matters have been considerably more complex. Maritta and Alun know this; Cathy and Anna too. And Leslie Preger now laments:

I see my brother building another bridge over the River Kwai. The trouble is that there's just no middle way with Jackie – and it's this zeal which will eventually wear him out. My view is that it really is enough now.

To which Jack is quick to retort:

But it's not enough, you see. Because if our clinics were to close, many of the patients would not get medical help of any kind. Yet that help is available – and I believe that the pavement-dwellers and destitutes of Calcutta have a moral right to receive it. The government say no and I say yes. That's why our campaign to get registration must continue. The official papers have still to come through. That's why we should all work together. Then, truly, mountains can be moved.

Travel to Middleton Row today, and the chances are that you will bump into Dr Jack, self-confessed oddball and still unregistered pavement practitioner of Calcutta. His patients remain the city's destitutes, the diseased and dispossessed, those who live and die on the streets. For many years now, through both the sweltering heat of the summer and the downpours of the monsoon, Jack has been seated on this modest patch of pavement, stethoscope casually slung around his neck, poking and prodding crowds of cripples. Thousands of case histories have been jotted down, tons of medicines distributed. One consequence of this is that the clinic is now more popular, its services more in demand, than ever before. And that is why mothers queue from the early hours of the morning to ensure that their new-born child might be given that additional and elusive boost, so that it might have a chance of emerging victorious in its fight for precious life in a city where the odds are stacked so heavily against it. For Dr Jack, there is still work to be done. Because the mountains of Calcutta have still to be moved.

Postscript

Anyone interested in sending a donation to support the work of Dr Jack Preger should make contact with one of the following organizations:

United Kingdom
Frances Sauven
Calcutta Rescue Fund
PO Box 52
Brentford
Middlesex TW 8PS

Belgium
Gerda Van Bueren
Du Chastellei 39
2060 Merksem

France
Calcutta Espoir
M. A. Massiani
10, rue croix des Petits Champs
750001 Paris

Calcutta Espoir
Vincent Cadiergue
2, Grande rue de la Guillotière
69007 Lyon

Calcutta Espoir
3, rue de Rimbach
67100 Strasbourg

Germany
Renate Hadasch
Forderverein Calcutta Rescue Clinic
Ludwig Richter Strasse 15
8 München 21

Spain
Raymond Deweert
Calcutta Esperanza
Calle Rayo No. 3
Urban 'Don Pedro'
29693 Estepona

Switzerland
Calcutta Espoir (Suisse)
2, ch. des Fleurettes
1860 Aigle

USA and Canada
Sven Thesen
Suite 108
6075 The Corners PKY
Norcross, GA 30092

Index

Index